INDIA'S DECADE *of* REFORMS

INDIA'S DECADE of REFORMS
RESERVE BANK OF INDIA AT CENTRAL STAGE

M G WARRIER

Notion Press

Old No. 38, New No. 6
McNichols Road, Chetpet
Chennai - 600 031

First Published by Notion Press 2018
Copyright © M G Warrier 2018
All Rights Reserved.

ISBN 978-1-64249-143-2

This book has been published with all reasonable efforts taken to make the material error-free after the consent of the author. No part of this book shall be used, reproduced in any manner whatsoever without written permission from the author, except in the case of brief quotations embodied in critical articles and reviews.

The Author of this book is solely responsible and liable for its content including but not limited to the views, representations, descriptions, statements, information, opinions and references ["Content"]. The Content of this book shall not constitute or be construed or deemed to reflect the opinion or expression of the Publisher or Editor. Neither the Publisher nor Editor endorse or approve the Content of this book or guarantee the reliability, accuracy or completeness of the Content published herein and do not make any representations or warranties of any kind, express or implied, including but not limited to the implied warranties of merchantability, fitness for a particular purpose. The Publisher and Editor shall not be liable whatsoever for any errors, omissions, whether such errors or omissions result from negligence, accident, or any other cause or claims for loss or damages of any kind, including without limitation, indirect or consequential loss or damage arising out of use, inability to use, or about the reliability, accuracy or sufficiency of the information contained in this book.

To
Sudha
Kiran, Reshmy
Smitha
Govind, Vihaan
and
All my well-wishers

Contents

S S Tarapore about M G Warrier   *ix*
Usha Thorat's comments   *xiii*
Preface   *xv*

Section I
Reserve Bank of India and Monetary Policy

Reserve Bank of India at 80 Plus	3
RBI's Role in Economic Development	15
Dr. Raghuram Rajan's Contribution	23
Monetary Policy I	29
Monetary Policy II	37
Monetary Policy Committee	46
Convergence of Fiscal and Monetary Policies	54

Section II
Note-Ban and After

Mainstreaming Cash Flows	67
A God-sent Opportunity to Cleanse the System	74
Indian Banking System: Safe, Secure and Trustworthy	87

Section III
Institutional Reforms

Banks' Mergers: Big is Beautiful!	101
A Holistic Approach to PSBs' Merger	110
Small Banks, Big Expectations	120
Back to Multi-Agency System	126
Bad Bank: Not a Good Idea?	134
Appendix 1	143
PSBs' Recapitalization Gets on Track	148
Appendix 2	155

Section IV
Stressed Assets in Indian Economy

Management of Stressed Bank Assets	159
Banking on Bankruptcy Law	168

Section V
Development Issues: Works in Progress

Gold Management in India	181
Universal Basic Minimum Income	188
Agricultural Income Tax	193
Politics and Economics of Farm Loan Waiver	196
National Pension System	203
Role of Auditors	217
Tourism: Under-exploited Potential	228

Section VI
Prologue as Epilogue

Eradicating Corruption: Power to The People	237

S S Tarapore about M G Warrier

M G Warrier's first book "Banking, Reforms & Corruption: Development Issues in 21st Century India" was published in 2014. S S Tarapore, Economist had this to say in his Foreword to the book:

Mumbai
February 12, 2014

Traditionally, central bankers have been reticent and generally stayed out of the public gaze. More recently, central bankers have been forthcoming and have engaged in public debate. Given these traditions, it is not surprising that most retired bankers do not air their views in the public domain.

In many ways Govinda Warrier is an exception in that he is ever willing to engage in public debate on issues of relevance to the common person. His interests are wide ranging, from monetary policy, banking and fiscal policy to HRD issues and senior citizens. He expresses his views with great conviction but with his predilection towards pragmatism which enables him to see a better way of conducting policy. His writings reflect the current economic debate and students, policy makers, opinion makers, bankers, economists and the discerning public would greatly benefit from reading this cameo of economic issues.

I hope that Warrier's efforts would encourage other retired central bankers to join the debate.

– **S S Tarapore**
Economist

Usha Thorat's Comments

Usha Thorat, Former Deputy Governor, Reserve Bank of India made these observations about M G Warrier and his book "Banking, Reforms & Corruption: Development Issues in 21st Century India" published in 2014:

I am not surprised and am certainly happy that M G Warrier has decided to bring out in a book form his writings on banking, economy and social issues over the last few years in newspapers and other media.

I have known Warrier since 1980's and apart from being extremely intelligent, I found him to have a very practical and mature approach to issues of policy and practice in RBI. His areas of interest has clearly expanded in his post-retirement period which has seen him as emerging as an observer of the national economy and society which he expresses through his writings – his concern for good governance in all matters are reflected in his commentaries on current issues and he is unafraid in articulating uncomfortable truths.

His reflections on policy matters have been perused by many of us when at the helm of policy and continue to attract interest. His style is crisp and direct and I would commend this book to all students teachers and common man interested in an independent and mature view.

– Usha Thorat

Preface

This book has depended mostly on articles written by me for magazines and newspapers during the last four years.

The book is in six sections. First two sections cover issues in which Reserve bank of India has mandated roles to play as banking regulator and manager of currency. After a recap of RBI's evolution as a unique central bank playing a major role in the country's economic development, Section I reviews the recent changes in monetary policy management. The stress is on the need for convergence of fiscal and monetary policies to promote overall economic development of the country.

Section II has three chapters on "Note-Ban and After" dwelling in some detail into the rationale behind withdrawal of high value currency notes from circulation, the impact of the measure and finally takes a look at the resilience of Indian Banking System despite neglect from owners and exploitation by the rich and the powerful.

Section III in four chapters gives a birds eye view of the emerging Multi-Agency System in the financial sector. Section IV examines Stressed Assets in Indian Economy and how GOI and RBI together are handling the challenges arising from them. Section V carries some essays opening debates on some development issues or issues affecting development.

Section VI has only one chapter under 'Prologue as Epilogue.' This is an adaptation from my article "Eradicating Corruption: Power to The People" published at moneylife. in on September 25, 2012.

– M G Warrier
November 24, 2017

*****

SECTION I

Reserve Bank of India and Monetary Policy

Reserve Bank of India at 80 Plus

Writing on Dr. Raghuram Rajan, on his appointment as RBI Governor, I had concluded my column in The Global ANALYST (September, 2013) with the following observation:

"To conclude, I must say, the appointment of Dr. Rajan has raised huge expectations. Can the new RBI governor help the economy, besieged by a plethora of challenges including a weakening currency, burgeoning deficits, sluggish growth, runaway inflation, rising interest costs, etc., regain momentum? Well, only time will tell."

Dr Rajan's efforts to restore people's confidence in the Indian Financial System have succeeded and there cannot be a better testimony for this than the appreciation showered on RBI and its governor by Prime Minister Narendra Modi on April 2, 2015 in Mumbai on the occasion of RBI's 81st birthday. Appreciating the role played by RBI over the last 80 years, the Prime Minister also complimented the RBI Governor Dr. Raghuram Rajan, for his grasp and clarity on economic issues. While RBI's professionalism and expertise which has placed the institution on a high pedestal among central banks, the following observation coming from Dr. Raghuram Rajan after 20 months stay inside the institution must boost the morale of all RBites (serving and retired). He said:

"The RBI is also respected for its integrity. It is a matter of great pride for me today that when someone enters our building to persuade us to change a regulation, they come armed not with money but with arguments about what is right. Let me conclude. Strong national institutions are hard to build. Therefore existing ones should be nurtured from the outside, and constantly rejuvenated from the inside, for there are precious few of them. In the 81st year of this great institution let us rededicate it to helping the nation secure prosperity and economic opportunity for all."

Eighty-first birthday, after watching 1000 full moons (as Prime Minister Modi said felicitating RBI for its achievements and the leadership provided by Dr. Raghuram Rajan at the seminar on Financial Inclusion organized in Mumbai on April 2, 2015) is an occasion for organizations like Reserve Bank of India to take stock of the achievements so far and bringing back the focus to its role expectations. This chapter makes an attempt to recap the milestones covered by the central bank so far.

Hilton Young Commission

The Hilton Young Commission, appointed in August 1925 'to examine and report on the Indian Exchange and Currency System and practice; to consider whether any modifications are desirable in the interests of India; and to make recommendations' though not mandated to examine the need for a central bank or State Bank examined this aspect and strongly recommended the establishment of a central bank to be called 'Reserve Bank of India' to which all central banking functions were to be entrusted.

Formative Years (1927–34)
The Gold Standard and Reserve Bank of India Bill introduced in the Legislative Assembly on January 25, 1927. As there was no agreement on several procedural and operational aspects concerning setting up of Reserve Bank, the Legislative assembly, after long deliberations, decided on September 8, 1927, not to proceed with passing of this bill. In January 1928, Government of India introduced another Bill almost on the same pattern, but this effort was also aborted midway on February 10, 1928. The proposal for establishing Reserve Bank of India got further impetus as part of constitutional reforms during the early 1930's. Indian Central Banking Enquiry Committee (1931) strongly recommended setting up of a 'Reserve bank' at the 'earliest possible date.' The foreign experts advising the Committee endorsed the recommendation observing: *"The paramount interests for the country involved in the establishment, within the shortest time possible, of such an independent institution, free from political influence, can hardly be over-estimated"*

Reserve Bank of India Act, 1934
The Reserve Bank Bill, 1933 introduced in the Legislative Assembly on September 8, 1933 finally received the assent of the Governor-General on March 6, 1934. Thus the Reserve bank of India came into being on April 1, 1935.

Having commenced functioning on April 1, 1935, Reserve Bank of India celebrated its 81st birthday on April 1, 2015. If one goes by the messages exchanged between the then Secretary of State for India and the Reserve bank of India Governor on the occasion of the inauguration of the Bank, looking back, the institution can be proud about having met the role expectations excellently well during the one thousand *chandramaasas* of its existence. To quote from the History of the Reserve Bank of India:

"On the occasion of the inauguration of the Bank, the Secretary of State for India sent the following message to the Governor:

As Reserve Bank commences active operations today I take opportunity to convey to you and your colleagues on the Board my most cordial good wishes and to express my confidence that this great undertaking will contribute largely to the economic well-being of India and of its people.

Replying on behalf of the Deputy Governors, the Board and himself, the Governor assured the Secretary of State,

That their utmost endeavour will be to promote the economic well-being of India and thereby completely justify the institution of the Reserve bank of India"

Early Years (1935–45)
During this period, Reserve bank focussed attention on core central banking funcions including issue of currency and monetary policy issues.

Regulation and Supervision (1945–54)
The period saw strengthening of Reserve Bank in its regulatory and supervisory roles empowered by the passing of Banking Companies Act, formation of State Bank of Pakistan, internal strengthening by creation of Department of Banking Development, introduction of Bill Market Scheme etc.

Institutions Building (1955–75)
The two decades saw developments like introduction of Deposit Insurance, Selective Credit Control, consolidation of banking sector (mainly merger/amalgamation of banks in the private sector), regulation of deposit acceptance activities of Non-Banking Finance Companies, bringing cooperative banks under the purview of Banking Regulation Act, nationalisation of scheduled commercial banks, passing of Foreign Exchange Regulation Act and introduction of Differential Interest rate Scheme.

Expansion of Banking Business and Thrust on Rural Credit (1975–95)
Several new monetary policy initiatives (like introduction of the concepts of M1, M2, M3), setting up of the National Bank for Agriculture and Rural Development under joint-ownership of GOI and RBI following the recommendations of CRAFFICARD report, setting up of BIFR, introduction of Agriculture and Rural Debt relief Scheme, 1990, successful management of external payment crisis of 1991, issue of guidelines for issue of new bank licences and nationalised banks entering capital market marked this period.

Recent Times: Managing Crises and Growing With Reforms (1995–2015)

The period saw interest rates deregulation, use of technology in a big way (RBI Website became operational in 1996), introduction of interim liquidity adjustment facility, Risk-based supervision of banks, more focus on financial inclusion and microfinance, subsidiarisation of foreign banks in India, deregulation of savings bank deposit rates, move to issue more banking licences for different categories of banks and more recently on February 20, 2015, the signing of an agreement between GOI and RBI on Inflation Targeting.

RBI's Autonomy

Central government has appointed two directors on Reserve Bank of India's Central Board in the place of one. The allegation is that the move aims at dominating the Board and stifling RBI's approach to policies. This will remain just an allegation as nothing prevents central government from ensuring that the entire board including the top management comprise only the government's 'yes men.' But RBI, due to some divine reason, has over time attained an institutional identity much superior to the combined 'net-worth' of individuals who manage the institution. It is unfortunate that efforts are being made, through commissioned reports, to equate RBI to SEBI and IRDA which have only limited regulatory/supervisory role on stock market and insurance market respectively, whereas RBI' responsibility includes ensuring economic growth with price stability, monetary stability which encompasses regulation of the entire financial system which comprises of various markets, institutions and products. The interference of the Government by way of issue of directives to banks directly and advising them or influencing them to tune to the central government's thinking is a trespass into RBI's supervisory and regulatory territory. RBI Governor has expressed his reservations against many of the recommendations of FSLRC which do not seem to have been taken seriously both by the government and the bureaucracy. The bureaucracy's ego and jealousy on RBI's professionalism, honesty and excellent reputation in the market for its non-corrupt practices should not lead to interference in the day-to-day administration and HRMD-related issues (like remuneration package and retirement benefits) of the central bank by GOI resulting in sagging morale of the RBI staff.

RBI's Internal Reserves

A related issue is strengthening the balance sheet of RBI by ploughing back a portion of surplus income to internal reserves, as was the practice till 2012–13 (there was an internally accepted target of 12 per cent of RBI balance sheet size, which was almost touched in 2009, but progressively slipped down later). A strong RBI balance sheet will give comfort to both GOI and RBI when fiscal and monetary policy initiatives affect inflow of income and/or result in a need to access internal reserves.

A recent media report mentioned that there has been no formal published study on the adequacy of reserves and RBI has been going by experiences. Every decision of RBI is based on close scrutiny of available information, though it may not be possible to create a 'model' which can be followed for the timing of buying and selling of dollar or internal debt management operations or for deciding the adequacy of the central bank's own internal reserves, or for that matter any individual monetary policy decision. The government should, in such a situation rely on the expertise and experience of RBI. It is in this context that successive RBI Governors and economists like S S Tarapore are making a plea to go slow on truncating the Indian central bank.

Forex Reserves Management

RBI with effective support from GOI has been managing India's forex reserves well and perhaps there was only one occasion when an alarming fall in reserves led to fire-fighting operations including pledging a portion of gold stock (which had to be physically carried abroad) to meet payment obligations.

In the recent past, after hovering around $300 billion for quite some time, there has been progressive accumulation in reserves during the last three years, raising total reserves to $341 billion by end-March 2015 and further to $400 billion in 2017. The cost worries on account of low return on foreign currency assets (less than 2 per cent per annum), expressed by RBI Governor sometime back, should not deter RBI and GOI making efforts to move towards the tentative foreign exchange reserves target of $750 to $ 1 trillion suggested by GOI's policy think tank, within a reasonable timeframe. RBI should also support the GOI budget initiatives aimed at better management of domestic gold stock by increasing the gold component in forex reserves without increase in gold import. This will need more efforts to mainstream domestic gold stock idling in several vaults including those with religious institutions.

Goi and RBI: Some Relationship Issues

It cannot be just coincidental, that while interacting with media on March 22, 2015 after addressing the 550th Central Board Meeting of the Reserve Bank of India, Finance Minister Arun Jaitley sought to dispel any talk of rift with RBI. He said: "There has always been and will continue to be a regular interaction between the Reserve Bank and the government... We have complete free and frank discussions, and therefore, there is no question of any disconnect. I have repeatedly clarified that." This reassurance, coming in the context of the Union Budget 2015–16, which contains certain announcements aimed at redefining the traditional relationship between GOI and RBI, need to be taken in the right spirit and welcomed, and GOI on their part need to be more visible in allowing statutory bodies to function with confidence within the mandated contours.

The views expressed by RBI Governor Dr. Raghuram Rajan about debt management, fiscal deficit and the measures to be initiated by central and state governments to improve environment to support economic development make sense and should be seen in right spirit. A reading together of the views of the Finance Minister and the RBI Governor gives one the comfort that the harmony in approach of GOI and RBI which existed in the initial days of RBI's functioning has been preserved and, definitely 'rift' is not the word to be used for explaining differences in views which are being discussed and settled from time to time.

There cannot be two views about the need for changes in institutional structure and procedures. Fortunately, like the Indian Railways, GOI and RBI have also taken up modernization seriously.

The need for comprehensive changes in the Reserve Bank of India Act, 1934 had been foreseen by the writers of the Act who included the following clauses in the Preamble of the Act:

"And Whereas in the present disorganization of the monetary systems of the world it is not possible to determine what is suitable as a permanent basis for the Indian monetary system;

But Whereas it is expedient to make temporary provision on the basis of the existing monetary system, and to leave the question of the monetary standard best suited to India to be considered when the international monetary position has become sufficiently clear and stable to make it possible to frame permanent measures;"

A god-sent opportunity for such a review was ignored by the Financial Sector Legislative Reforms Commission (FSLRC) which opted to re-invent structures and legislative instruments to help out a government from embarrassment caused by a weak finance ministry (not a weak Finance Minister) not equipped to argue its cases sensibly with statutory bodies and corporates.

Public Debt Management Agency

As the word 'rift' was used by media in the context of transfer of public debt management responsibility from RBI to another 'independent' agency, a short discussion of the proposal will be in order.

Intentions behind the proposal for an independent Public Debt Management Agency 'outside' RBI and GOI may be noble. The institutional structure and policy approach of 1940's (the aggregate market borrowings of the government of India from 1940–41 to 1945–46 was Rs. 1,157 crore and in the fiscal year 2017–18, GOI borrowing programme may touch a high of Rs. 6 lakh crore!) did not undergo any comprehensive revamp during later times and there will be no two views on the need for an overhaul, as the present needs are different.

Within RBI the skill development and acquisition of expertise for managing the core functions have been an ongoing process. But, beyond expertise, ultimately, as the agency will have to handle 'debt' which is dependent on credibility and clout of the borrower, for the moment, it is better to continue status quo. Every time a new initiative or decision is taken affecting financial sector, we have a legacy of vested interests trying to tilt the decision in their favour by putting a wedge between GOI and RBI. It is comforting to see that in recent years RBI and Finance Ministry have understood the game and are working in tandem.

For several reasons, it would be expedient to allow RBI to continue public debt management at least for another decade. One, there is no retail market for government securities and therefore government borrowing is dependent on commercial banks (which are mandated to maintain a certain percentage of their assets in 'cash, gold or unencumbered approved securities...') and financial institutions.

Two, Reserve Bank of India has been managing public debt for several years well and this has helped the institution develop in-house expertise and skill which cannot be easily 'transferred' to a new organization. Three, there is no guarantee that a new agency will be in a position to function independent of GOI and RBI for reasons One and Two!

As RBI and Finance Ministry are on the same page in regard to having an independent Public Debt Management Agency, perhaps GOI could consider setting up a statutory body to initially handle management of surplus funds and borrowings of public sector organizations, management of state government borrowings (now being handled by RBI on an agency basis (Section 21A of RBI Act) and such other responsibilities GOI may entrust to that organization. As the organization grows, it can help in building a retail market for government securities and gradually relieve RBI of public debt management responsibilities.

*****

RBI's Role in Economic Development

Recent times have witnessed debates in both the print and electronic media on the role of central bank's policy intervention in promoting economic growth in India. These were, at times part of criticism against Reserve Bank of India, sometimes part of articles supported by deep analysis of various components of economic growth indicators and more often academic discussions by economists and politicians with diverse backgrounds and constituency interests. Here we attempt to discuss, how best the system can take advantage of the change of guard in New Delhi to harmonize the handling of inflation and growth by Reserve Bank of India and central government.

One aspect which most of the analysts and critiques usually ignore is that the central bank (RBI) mandated to administer monetary policy has limited instruments to tame inflation and political decisions like those about administered prices, subsidy, waiver of taxes and dues to government and banks and so on taken by central and state governments sometimes set off whatever little is done by RBI to manage inflation. Therefore, Government of India should keep this in view and at least in the immediate future be magnanimous in extending fiscal policy support to RBI initiatives.

From this perspective, the finance minister who had all the freedom to take off from a fresh launch pad could factor in some of the following thoughts while he moves on to convert the election promises and the expectations of 'WE THE PEOPLE' who have opted for a change – 2014 vote was for a change and any other interpretation based on politics, religion or minority/majority or left/right can only generate ill-will and controversies – into hard figures in his financial planning, in his budgets year after year:

Agriculture

Agriculture deserves more attention from planners and policy makers, not just on the eve of annual Budgets. This is a neglected sector for historic reasons. GOI should look at agriculture not only from the angles of farm sector production, but food security and the millions of agricultural laborers who cannot migrate to urban areas also. In the changed scenario, there is need to project agriculture as a sector which should graduate to self-supporting stage viewed from a 'business' point of view. This will need:

- Land reforms including need-based cultivation of crops required for consumption and export/commercial purposes
- Change in the approach to agricultural income and taxation thereof
- Nationalization of idle lands which can be used for cultivation or commercial/infrastructure purposes.
- Re-look at food stocks and their utilization as also support prices and costs and benefits of public distribution systems across states.

Pay – Back Time for Super-Rich

RBI Governors have been all along articulating the central bank's expectations from the finance ministry by way of fiscal policy support for central bank initiatives to tame inflation. As time is running out let us think differently and suggest some one-time measures which GOI could consider:

i. Steps to price land and other resources being 'gifted' to corporates and rich individuals under various pretexts at market rates and plan recovery of costs as and when such 'gifts' start giving return

ii. A one-time surcharge on income tax payable by super-rich and create a rolling fund for financing social sector (The indicative Corporate Social Responsibility expenditure at 2 percent of surplus income is ridiculously low).

iii. According to one assessment, a ten per cent surcharge on the tax payable by taxpayers who report an annual income of more than Rs. 1 million will fetch about Rs. 110 billion in a full financial year. As the last few years have been more strenuous for those with annual income level below Rs. 1 million and that category deserves some 'cross-subsidization' from the super-rich, GOI should consider a surcharge in annual budgets, on the tax payable by those with income above Rs. 1 million. The rate of such surcharge could be 10 to 20 per cent depending on policy perceptions. This surcharge collection should be ear-marked for creating a corpus for 'additional' funding of social sector which has been neglected in recent years. The 'below moderate' rise in plan expenditure, at 6% over the previous year during recent years, shows the saturation level of GOI's capacity to mobilize resources for social sector, within the budgetary framework. But this should not dishearten the government. Money is accumulating outside the government fold, almost with the same speed at which heaps of garbage are growing in cities and suburbs. It is government's responsibility to canalize such hoardings for productive purposes. Even if money outside government accounts are not accounted in the budget, GOI's guidance expressed through Budget Speech should be clear about the social responsibility of people who 'grow' exploiting nation's resources. Perhaps the responsibility to develop infrastructure for healthcare, transport, education, old age care and so on in geographical areas close to large industrial establishments could be entrusted to the industrialists concerned. Tata has been doing this voluntarily in certain areas.

National Pension System

Abolish National Pension System (NPS). This will absolve employers' commitment to make 'matching contribution.' As financial position improves, employers including GOI should create pension funds to honor future commitments. Simultaneously, the Employees Provident Organization should be strengthened and the scheme implemented by that organization made more popular, integrating the essential rationale for introduction of NPS.

External Compulsions

India need not buy all the 'products' coming the country's way from rating agencies and brokerages whose allegiance is more towards 'developed world' which is struggling to keep its head above neck-deep debt and other problems including stagnation in growth since a few years. GOI should look for India-specific solutions for India-specific problems. As the country is at a different stage of development, we should stop worrying about the comparative figures of growth rates, savings rates, return on investment or inflation in countries like USA or Australia. Same holds true about SLR norms for banks and GOI dependence on captive sources like SLR. GOI should not hesitate to subsidize social sector or at least improve funding of social sector (including nutrition/food security, education, healthcare and poverty eradication) even at the cost of other sectors as the dwindling resources flow is impacting further development.

Interest Rate Subsidy

Stop subsidizing interest rates on loans for any purpose including agriculture beyond reasonable levels. Fancy schemes like zero-interest rate loans and 'free' rations should be discouraged and financial support to eligible categories should be given in a transparent manner. Recalcitrant states should be made to fall in line through appropriate disincentives.

The word '**subsidy**,' because of the way in which it is being used by economists, analysts and planners, has got a bad reputation in India. When flowers were destroyed in Holland market to manage prices, or costs of cultivation were supported in US to ensure production of certain commodities, or food coupons were given at reduced rates or free of cost to certain classes of people in developed countries, there was no hue and cry over the cost to the taxpayer or 'subsidy' factored in, in different forms. So long as a rational costs-prices-wages-income policy is not in place, so long as starvation wages, unemployment and under-employment remain at ugly levels, any government, irrespective of changes in political alignments will not be able to go ahead with reforms just to support the upper middle class and rich people who account for less than 20% of India's population. 'Subsidy' will resurface in one form or the other.

Taming Inflation

For taming inflation or plainly to retain prices within acceptable levels, long-term planning, regulatory support and coordinated efforts by government and stakeholders in the market and better consumer-awareness may have to get much more attention than they are getting now. Periodic wide fluctuations in onion prices are one indicator to show how those who gain control over stocks of goods that have a longer shelf-life manipulate prices. The government may not need an economist to tell that the position of demand and supply has an impact on prices. Procurement by processing industry and wholesalers who have ongoing responsibility to maintain supplies to retail outlets like departmental stores and supply-chains, purchase by affluent pockets/states within the country which can afford to pay higher prices and export commitments affect prices of vegetables, meat and eggs. A long-term policy on the food front may have to factor in improving productivity of land under cultivation, encouraging multiple-cropping patterns wherever feasible, ensuring remunerative farm-gate prices, estimating in advance the state-wise requirements for consumption, processing and export and regulating inter-state movements taking into account the potential for increasing local production. For such a change in approach, grass-root-level planning by sharing responsibility with state governments and local self-government bodies has to become a reality. There is a limit up to which sermons and directives from Delhi can help improve the position.

The managers of fiscal and monetary policy cannot be blamed as inflation is only one of the indicators that tell them the results of various fiscal and monetary policy measures they initiate. Depending on the direction they look, they are always able to either venture an optimistic prediction or tell us where either of them need correct the next step. This partly explains the ongoing debate among economists, bankers and political leadership about the direction monetary and fiscal policies should take. Problem is also about various categories of inflation, the methods of calculation of inflation and how the inflation (CPI or WPI inflation, for instance) affect different sectors of economy and different income-groups. There is no clarity or uniformity in perspective on such things among those who are responsible to prescribe corrective measures. The 'Inflation elephant' is perceived as a different monster by scholars from different schools of economics depending on their social and academic background and in which geographical area they live.

Inflation Targeting (IT)

The best conclusion for this chapter could be a quote from my former colleague Dr. Charan Singh who is *the RBI Chair Professor of Economics at the Indian Institute of Management, Bangalore:*

"Historically, IT (Inflation Targeting) has been generally adopted by countries recording hyperinflation. In India, that has never been the case. Therefore, inflicting such high interest rates on the Indian public in the name of combating inflation has only resulted in lower investment and growth, and higher non-performing assets. In view of the young population of India, our priorities should probably be on ensuring higher employment and growth and not just low inflation."

Without disagreeing, I would add that inflation need to be maintained at tolerable levels, to maintain stability in cost of living for those who do not have 'savings' to fall upon to subsidize expenses as prices fluctuate to their disadvantage!

*****

Dr. Raghuram Rajan's Contribution

Writing about Dr. Raghuram Rajan in September 2013(He had taken charge as RBI Governor on September 4, 2013) in The Global ANALYST (TGA), I had observed:

"The present focus on financial inclusion and taming inflation which are incidentally in tune with the vision expressed by the Governor-Designate Dr. Rajan is consistent with the tradition maintained by RBI.

Once he gets a feel of the constraints with which RBI has been having a tight rope walk in harmonizing the monetary policy in the recent past with the unbridled fiscal policy guided by the pulls and pushes of a coalition government at the Centre, Rajan is unlikely to toe the GOI line on fiscal deficit and Current Account Deficit, particularly that of the Finance Minister. As a corollary, Finance Minister Chidambaram may not find an RBI Governor who will support his pet project FSLRC (Financial Sector Legislative Reforms Commission) which has produced a report aimed at making RBI a 'department' of the Finance Ministry."

After Dr. Rajan returned to academia on completion of his 3 year tenure, while writing on the Monetary Policy Committee in the November 2016 issue of TGA, I said:

Contrary to the expectations of ordinary humans like this writer who criticized the attempt by the Financial Sector Legislative Reforms Commission (FSLRC) for writing a monologue report on dotted lines to satisfy certain vested interests, brushing aside all dissents even from within the Commission, we now find that the FSLRC report is being used as just a reference point for initiating long overdue reforms in the financial sector. The whole credit for this change of mindset in the finance ministry should go to one individual Dr. Raghuram G Rajan, who appeared on the scene at the right time and like an *avatar,* disappeared from the scene after almost completing his mission in about three years.

One is compelled to recall S S Tarapore's May 2013 observations on FSLRC:

"The Commission recommends the setting up of a statutory Monetary Policy Committee (MPC) to take executive decisions on monetary policy with each member having a vote and the Chairperson having a veto, which must be explained with a public statement. The devil is in the detail.

There would be only two RBI members and five external members appointed by the Government. The Ministry of Finance nominee would be a non-voting member on the MPC but would articulate the Government viewpoint. With Big Brother watching over their shoulder, brave would be the external member who would deviate from the Government line. The RBI would be better off with the present arrangement.

The leitmotif of the FSLRC is to charge the gate of the temple of money with iconoclastic fervor. One prays that in this internecine battle, RBI's Pretorian Guards fight off the charge of the Commissioners. One must remember that countries that destroy their central banks destroy themselves."

Tarapore retired as Deputy Governor, RBI some twenty years ago. But post-retirement, literally till his last breath, he remained a watchdog of the rights and responsibilities of the central bank which he served for more than three decades. His writings and speeches during the last two decades can easily be prescribed as a treasure of teachings on policy formulation and implementation by RBI.

It is unfortunate that Tarapore did not live to see the changes that RBI under the able leadership of Dr. Rajan could bring about in the concept of MPC. In effect, while the RBI Governor is now unburdened of the individual responsibility of deciding on Monetary Policy, the central bank could get the existing arrangement of Technical Advisory Committee legalized and professionalized.

Hopefully, sooner than later, India will get the benefit of Dr. Rajan's presence back home and his participation in the country's effort to capture a status as a developed country within a couple of decades.

Dr. Raghuram Rajan's book "I Do What I Do: On Reform, Rhetoric and Resolve" released in September, 2017 and his speeches and interactions following and preceding the book release, to be precise, from September 4, 2017, the day he came out to speak after a one year self-imposed silence (claimed to be not to embarrass his successor Dr. Urjit Patel while settling down as governor!) are becoming food and fodder for a hungry media and starved analysts. The euphoria is likely to last much longer than the interest generated by two memoirs published in quick succession by his two illustrious predecessors at Mint Road, namely Dr. Duvvuri Subbarao and Dr. Y V Reddy in that order.

We will not attempt a review of Rajan's book at this stage for two reasons. One, the content of the book comprise speeches he delivered and articles he wrote, which, we have read only very recently, except for explanatory notes prefixed and suffixed by the author to explain the context and add clarity. Two, the interviews given by Rajan and the reviews already published make another recap of the content of the book or comments thereon redundant. We will restrict the scope of this chapter to select observations by Dr. Rajan himself about the book and comment on two or three select questions he has/should have asked himself about his performance as governor for which he has not been able to provide satisfactory answers.

Dr. Raghuram Rajan, with his long teaching experience and deep knowledge of the ins and outs of Indian financial sector, has been using his excellent communication skills ever since he started taking interest in India's economic development. Viewed in this context, his new book "I Do What I Do," which comes out without much delay after his return to academia, will be more popular among economists, analysts and policy makers than the memoirs his two immediate predecessors brought out in quick succession in recent years.

"I Do What I Do" interprets events during the three year tenure of the author's stay at Mint Road by just adding notes or explanations to what Dr. Rajan has already spoken or written as RBI governor.

Demonetization

The cautious observation about short-term economic costs outweighing long-term benefits of demonetization now being made public is a masterstroke. As the opinion was given 'orally,' it is always possible to play with the words like long term benefits and short term losses. The present observation makes it abundantly clear that RBI was associating with the groundwork for demonetization from February 2016. The present revelations can also expose Dr. Rajan to the allegation of having evaded the responsibility of getting himself involved in preparing RBI adequately to implement the 'Note ban,' once a decision was taken by GOI.

RBI's Capital and Reserves

Rajan remained a mere spectator when the central bank's capital and reserves eroded to an all time low during his tenure. Depending on an internal report which said RBI had "adequate reserves for three years" he saw the transfer of entire surplus income of RBI to GOI from 2013–14 to 2015–16. Result: The percentage of reserves to total assets came down from a self-set target of 12 percent of balance sheet total which the Bank had almost touched in 2009, to a low of 7.5 percent in 2015–16.

Parity of Pensionary Benefits for RBI Retirees With GOI

Dr. Rajan's having shown pedestrian apathy to the cause of parity with central government staff in retirement benefits for RBI retirees, is intriguing, as, on record (from RBI Annual Report 2014–15) he was convinced about the genuineness of the long-pending demand from the staff. On page 211 of his book, Dr. Rajan laments:

"...On the internal front, my biggest regret is that I could not solve a long-pending matter that I inherited from my predecessors: securing for retired RBI staff the same pension benefits that government employees enjoy, despite repeated assurances from the government that the matter would be addressed. I hope the government will do the right thing here..."

On His Return to Academia

As always, Dr. Rajan has pre-empted his adversaries from reading between the lines. Dr. Rajan's opponents have spread many stories in the media about his exit on completion of his "sanctioned leave." One year after leaving RBI, he himself also spoke about the absence of "offer on the table," while everyone knows his one foot was all through in Chicago!

Credit Should Go to Rajan

Rajan's contribution to sorting out some of the long-pending relationship issues between Government of India and the Reserve Bank of India and expediting banking sector reforms will be remembered in India with gratitude.

*****

Monetary Policy I

Every monetary policy review by Reserve Bank of India (RBI) is preceded by speculations about changes in policy repo rate and succeeded by different, and sometimes divergent views on what is stated in the RBI Governor's policy announcement through the monetary policy statement. The third Bi-monthly Monetary Policy Statement, 2015–16 was no exception. Monetary and Liquidity Measures announced by RBI Governor Dr. Raghuram Rajan said:

"On the basis of an assessment of the current and evolving macroeconomic situation, it has been decided to:
- keep the policy repo rate under the liquidity adjustment facility (LAF) unchanged at 7.25 per cent;
- keep the cash reserve ratio (CRR) of scheduled banks unchanged at 4.0 per cent of net demand and time liability (NDTL);
- continue to provide liquidity under overnight repos at 0.25 per cent of bank-wise NDTL at the LAF repo rate and liquidity under 14-day term repos as well as longer term repos of up to 0.75 per cent of NDTL of the banking system through auctions; and

- continue with daily variable rate repos and reverse repos to smooth liquidity.

Consequently, the reverse repo rate under the LAF will remain unchanged at 6.25 per cent, and the marginal standing facility (MSF) rate and the Bank Rate at 8.25 per cent."

The assessment that followed explained the background in which these decisions were taken. Governor, after explaining the global scenario, mentioned that in India, the economic recovery was still work in progress. Governor noted that headline consumer price index (CPI) inflation rose for the second successive month in June 2015 to a nine-month high on the back of a broad based increase in upside pressures, belying consensus expectations. The sharp month-on-month increase in food and non-food items overwhelmed the sizable 'base effect' in that month. Food inflation rose 60 basis points over the preceding month, driven by a spike in prices of vegetables, protein items – especially pulses, meat and milk – and spices.

According to RBI assessment, liquidity conditions had been very easy in June and July. A seasonal reduction in demand for currency and increased spending by Government coupled with structural factors such as low credit deployment relative to the volume of deposit mobilization contributed to surplus conditions in the money markets. This resulted in a significantly lower average daily net liquidity injection under the fixed rate repos under LAF, and variable rate term repo/reverse repo and MSF at 477 billion in June, down from 1031 billion in May. In July 2015 there was net absorption of 120 billion through these facilities.

In response to the reduction in the policy repo rate in June the weighted average call rate eased from 7.47 per cent in May to 7.11 per cent in June.

In the context of a plea for more 'cuts' from several quarters, the following observation in the policy statement referred to above were relevant:

"Since the first rate cut in January, the median base lending rates of banks has fallen by around 30 basis points, a fraction of the 75 basis points in rate cut so far. As loan demand picks up in Q3 of 2015–16, banks will see more gains from cutting rates."

Reserve Bank of India's Role

Having accepted an inflation target with an upper limit of 6%, RBI Governor's expression of intention to consider measures, that he thought may have an adverse impact on inflation, only when he was sure about inflation remaining within manageable level/s, should not normally surprise anyone.

In every discussion before and after monetary policy announcement, media and analysts, by habit, have been going round and round on 'rate cut' and this time around a couple of proposals in the (Draft) Indian Financial Code (IFC) circulated by GOI added spice to the debates.

In this context, RBI Governor Dr. Rajan's observation that as these need legislative changes, it may take years to materialize was a studied one. While the main text of the (Draft) IFC (now in circulation) has 94 chapters in over 200 pages, the major public controversy and debate surrounds only the composition of Monetary Policy Committee. People have started forgetting a more damaging proposal to rush through procedures to transfer the responsibility of Public Debt Management from RBI by setting up another body called Public Debt Management Agency (PDMA) directly under Ministry of Finance.

Minister of State (Finance) in another context mentioned that MPC issue forms only 3% of IFC (perhaps by word count!). He is right. IFC is an aggregation of duties and responsibilities of several agencies which have statutory functions in the financial sector. Now, the only way to handle it with responsibility would be to disaggregate it into manageable pieces covering different areas hitherto covered by different legislations. E. g. the areas covered by Reserve Bank of India Act, 1934 could be taken up first.

The other 'political' option would be to rush through some procedures and pass a wholesale legislation without much deliberation, on a convenient day. But that would be perilous for the country's financial sector and the Indian economy.

Having said that one takes note of the elegance with which RBI Governor Dr. Raghuram Rajan and Minister of State (Finance) Jayant Sinha fielded questions on the controversies arising from the proposals contained in the Draft Indian Financial Code circulated by Finance Ministry about composition of Monetary Policy Committee (MPC) during the first week of August 2015. Perhaps this expression of mutual trust and patience to listen to a different view other than one's own is worth emulating by the political leadership in Delhi on umpteen other disputes coming up every other day.

Both did not make any new revelations, but emphasized the need for mutual trust. While Sinha tried to differentiate between proposals and conclusions, Dr. Rajan fielded the question on MPC arguing that if veto power is retained, it doesn't change status quo. But Governor did not forget to acknowledge the respect with which GOI treated RBI all along. By asserting that RBI had always enjoyed de facto independence in policy formulation, he has also indicated, where the buck stops, in regard to monetary policy.

Referring to the efforts of GOI to 'cage' RBI's role, columnist T C A Srinivasa-Raghavan mentioned that RBI was a 'fly in the bottle.' In reality, RBI happens to be the "Curd in the Pot," if at all an analogy was needed to explain RBI's position. There has been unending disputes about whether curd is dependent on the pot for its existence or whether the pot gets value addition because it contains curd (*Thakrasyaadhaaram Ghatam vaa Ghatasyaadhaaram Thakram?*). Government and people of India, like the pot, are dependent on the central bank for retaining the health and strength of the economy.

Y V Reddy's oft-quoted observation that the contours of RBI's autonomy is decided by government cannot be disputed. But stifling a statutory organization's functional autonomy within the pre-decided mandates, by back-seat-driving by any force, brings down the reputation of both the institution and the owner, in this case GOI. RBI's autonomy or independence of monetary authority within the contours of government policy is not an issue just affecting those at the helm of the central bank.

The political leadership's selfish interest to have birds of passage at the helm of all limbs of governance, which will parrot the views of the day's government, which finds expression through measures like ensuring government-nominee domination on boards and committees, is a disturbing phenomenon, and needs to be curbed.

Mythili Bhusnurmath writing in Economic Times mentioned that sometimes monetary policy statements do not get the attention they deserve. One has to concede that not much is talked about the implications of various moves by RBI to manage monetary environment, beyond interest rates. Even the Financial Sector Legislative Reforms Commission (FSLRC) report and its off-shoot, the (Draft) Indian Financial Code are being micro-analyzed only around RBI's role in deciding base interest rates, whereas the code attempts to reinvent every financial regulator!

Former RBI Deputy Governor Usha Thorat in an article in the Indian Express has brilliantly argued the case for not rushing through the IFC at this stage. Economist and former Deputy Governor S S Tarapore had consistently argued the need to preserve the present strength and capabilities of RBI in policy formulation unscathed.

Back on IFC, let us trust the commitment given by both the ministers, Jaitley and Sinha, when they said they are open on IFC, would be honoured. FSLRC report need to be revisited, giving a second reading together with the notes of dissent and the relevance of the recommendations in the present Indian context. Especially because, dissent within the Commission was handled roughly by the Chairman and even the brief dissenting notes recorded by members of the Commission did not get the attention they deserved. There is need for fresh debate for which the observations made by the two former Deputy Governors mentioned earlier can form the basis.

RBI's autonomy or independence of monetary authority within the contours of government policy is not an issue just affecting those at the helm of the central bank. The stability of India's financial sector and the country's image outside are dependent on that.

The excellent, crisp analysis by the former RBI Deputy Governor, Usha Thorat in her article "A Code too soon" published in The Hindu Business Line on July 30, 2015, incidentally, reflected the thinking of those who are aware of the evolution of RBI as a performing central bank in the Indian context. This institution cannot be compared with central banks in other countries with limited central banking functions. GOI has been dependent on RBI on several occasions in the past for coming out of tricky situations. It is not accidental that GOI, irrespective of political colour, has been ensuring strong leadership for RBI.

Pradeep S Mehta writing in the Hindu Business Line (August 7, 2015) depending on an observation by 20th Century common law judge Lord Denning who preferred dwelling into the unknown to status quo argued strongly for going ahead with formalizing the (Draft) IFC circulated by finance ministry. Mehta concluded that 'no power on earth must be allowed to stop reforms in India,' which view no power in India can dispute!

But I beg to differ on Mehta's view that the Code (the Indian Financial Code in the form now in circulation) must be urgently adopted. India was inspired when Prime Minister Modi, speaking from the ramparts of Red Fort on August 15, 2014, said that Planning Commission was a house in disrepair and he proposed to rebuild it instead of wasting resources on repair and maintenance. He could put in place NITI *Aayog* without dismantling Planning Commission. Indian judiciary, India's legislations including those covered by Financial Sector Legislative Reforms Commission (FSLRC) report and, perhaps, the entire architecture now in place for governance are awaiting comprehensive overhaul.

The office of Indian President, the Election Commission, CAG, RBI and the Supreme Court are some of the limbs which have withstood the test of time during the last 70 years since independence. In their case, the assertion by Lord Denning that 'the law will stand still' does not hold good, as these institutions had fairly good leadership all along, capable of application of mind, which helped them grow to meet the challenges they faced from time to time. Any initiative to reform them should take into account the evolution of their role so far. We must ensure that replacements are better than what is available now. The content of (Draft) IFC, unfortunately, does not give any assurance of the kind.

GOI should hurry slowly, if it does not want India to follow Greece, too soon!

*****

Monetary Policy II

In December 2015, The Global Analyst Managing Editor N Janardhan Rao mentioned to me about a media report which quoted a view that monetary policy is losing its sting with every incremental rise in money supply generating less growth each passing year. The report was padded further with observations like, "In FY15, every incremental rupee of money supply generated just Rs. 1.2 of incremental gross domestic product (GDP). The ratio was 1.6x in early 2000s and 2.2x on the eve of economic reforms in 1991 according to data from the Reserve Bank of India (RBI)."

As I have not done much research on the impact of monetary policy *per se* on GDP, adjusted for inflation over time, I am not disputing the content of the media report. But the report, which gives an impression that the function of central banks hovers around making adjustments in their own 'base rates,' is 'food for thought,' strong enough to make one get disturbed about the perception even among the well-informed people about monetary policy and the role of central bank in the economic growth of the country.

At the risk of repetition, we may have to dwell in some detail about the evolution of the role of Reserve Bank of India as an institution responsible for not only the core functions of a central bank, but as a proactive partner with Government of India in regulating and preserving a financial system which has been playing an effective role in the country's economic development.

At this stage, we need to go back in time. The Indian legislatures, during the two decades each that preceded and succeeded independence, functioned smoothly and gave shape to several statutes including the Indian Constitution and the Reserve Bank of India Act, 1934 which every Indian can be proud of. There were informed and intelligent debates in legislatures and the Constituent Assembly before finalizing every clause of the documents which later became statutes. The credit for this goes to the then political leadership, which did not have an opposition which thought its only role was to 'oppose,' and the Indian National Congress which respected and allowed 'informed dissent' from within and shared views with and took into confidence on all important issues, an opposition which had great leaders, but was not very strong, going by numbers.

We will leave this here, but the reminder was necessary to explain the context in which we are going back to the preamble of the Reserve Bank of India Act, 1934 for initiating a discussion on Monetary Policy. The PREAMBLE reads:

"PREAMBLE

An Act to constitute a Reserve Bank of India.

Whereas it is expedient to constitute a Reserve Bank for India **to regulate the issue of Bank notes and the keeping of reserves with a view to securing monetary stability in India and generally to operate the currency any credit system of the country to its advantage;**

And whereas in the present disorganisation of the monetary systems of the world it is not possible to determine what will be suitable as a permanent basis for the Indian monetary system;

But whereas it is expedient to make temporary provision on the basis of the existing monetary system, and to leave the question of the monetary standard best suited to India to be considered when the international monetary position has become sufficiently clear and stable to make it possible to frame permanent measures; It is hereby enacted as follows:"

Although, it would be illogical to presume that 'the international monetary position' did not 'become sufficiently clear and stable to make it possible to permanent measures' during the 8 decades that followed the establishment of RBI, fact remains that no comprehensive review of the provisions of RBI Act was ever taken up and this defies commonsense. Please do not remind me about the (Draft) Indian Financial Code (IFC) prepared by the Financial Sector Legislative Reforms Commission (FSLRC). The FSLRC lacked the expertise and time to undertake the huge task of reviewing the entire legislative set up in the Indian financial sector. The (Draft) IFC it put together is an *avial* (reference is to a South Indian mixed vegetable dish, which was originally prepared from the left-over vegetables after use for the main course menu for a feast!) cooked in a hurry by an amateur cook who did not have any idea about the final product or the fate of those who are destined to taste it. Suffice to conclude that the review envisaged in the original statute which constituted India's central bank is yet to happen. I am not contesting the use of FSLRC report as a basis for further deliberations on the issues that have been covered in the report.

By traditional definition, "Monetary Policy is a regulatory policy by which the central bank or monetary authority of a country controls the supply of money, availability of bank credit and cost of money, that is, the rate of Interest." Monetary management, therefore, is regarded as an important tool of economic management in India. RBI controls the supply of money and bank credit. The Central bank is duty-bound to see that legitimate credit requirements are met and at the same credit is not used for unproductive and speculative purposes. Reserve Bank of India is aware of this responsibility and rightly calls its credit policy as one of controlled expansion, with focus on economic development and financial inclusion. The constraints in evolving an ideal monetary policy emanates from the fact that the central bank is owned by Government of India which has huge stakes in public sector commercial banks which have a share of over 70 per cent in the country's banking business. Sometimes, GOI exercise their 'ownership rights' indirectly to manipulate the decisions of RBI and banks, which should normally be taken by the respective institutions, applying mind, consistent with the statutory mandate vested in these institutions.

The main objective of Monetary Policy in India is 'growth with stability.' This is sought to be achieved by regulating availability, cost and use of credit. Reserve Bank of India has also been playing a significant role in institution building in the financial sector. Even the recent approach of RBI to licensing a couple of new private sector banks and introducing payment banks and small banks which essentially meant bringing some of the existing institutions like post offices and microfinance institutions into mainstream banking business with concomitant obligation to conform to regulatory norms applicable to banks, should be seen in this perspective.

Financial stability means the ability of the economy to absorb shocks and maintain confidence in financial system. Threats to financial stability can come from internal and external shocks. Such shocks can destabilize the country's financial system. Thus, RBI adopts an apparently conservative policy approach seeking to maintain confidence in financial system through proper regulation and controls, without sacrificing the objective of growth. To be successful in its objectives, RBI needs functional independence within the contours of law and a strong balance sheet with adequate 'reserves' to meet any eventuality arising from its market-related operations in Indian and foreign currencies. RBI should also be in a position to manage its personnel by hiring competent staff and retaining them by providing competitive compensation and career development opportunities. Governor Dr. Raghuram Rajan has flagged some HR-related issues in RBI Annual Report 2014–15 which should receive the attention of GOI.

For historic reasons RBI has been involved also in ensuring adequate credit flow to priority sector which includes agriculture, export and small scale enterprises and weaker section of population. RBI guides banks to provide timely and adequate credit at affordable cost to weaker sections and low income groups.

Monetary policy helps in employment generation by influencing the rate of investment and allocation of investment among various economic activities of different labour intensities.

Interest Rates

The whole world starts worrying with concern whenever Fed Reserve considers any change in its benchmark rate. RBI had during 2015–16, till third quarter, reduced its base rate by 125 basis points. During the Monetary policy review on December 1, 2015, RBI Governor Dr. Rajan mentioned that reduction in benchmark rates by banks consequent to this had till then been to the extent 0.6 percentage points. The delay in percolation of the impact of RBI's rate cuts had made RBI think in terms of guiding banks to introduce 'marginal cost pricing.' In this context, Dr. Rajan referred to LIBOR (London Interbank Offered Rate) which, banks in UK charge each other for short term loans. The new concept of marginal cost pricing envisaged banks to pass on the benefits of deposit/resources cost reduction to their new borrowers immediately.

FSLRC and Monetary Policy Committee

The deliberations that preceded the constitution of the Monetary Policy Committee and the final recognition that as regards monetary policy management, the buck stops at RBI Governor's desk gave an impression that relationship issues between finance ministry and RBI should be sorted out first. In this context, let me recall

S S Tarapore's article 'A Plot to Destroy RBI' (The Hindu Business Line, May 3, 2013) which concluded with the following observations:

"Devil in the Detail

The Commission recommends the setting up of a statutory Monetary Policy Committee (MPC) to take executive decisions on monetary policy with each member having a vote and the Chairperson having a veto, which must be explained with a public statement. The devil is in the detail.

There would be only two RBI members and five external members appointed by the Government. The Ministry of Finance nominee would be a non-voting member on the MPC but would articulate the Government viewpoint.

With Big Brother watching over their shoulder, brave would be the external member who would deviate from the Government line. The RBI would be better off with the present arrangement.

The *leitmotif* of the FSLRC is to charge the gate of the temple of money with iconoclastic fervour. One prays that in this internecine battle, the RBI's Pretorian Guards fight off the charge of the Commissioners.

One must remember that countries that destroy their central banks destroy themselves."

Fortunately, times have changed and the change of guard at North Block (Finance Ministry) and Mint Road (RBI) has made mutual consultations between the central bank and GOI more frequent and meaningful. For those who have been following the position taken by some of the members of FSLRC and by the RBI top management, this gives great relief. The relief came also from the confidence that Dr. Rajan's strong leadership in the financial sector could defend the right postures consistently taken by the central bank.

Not much research is needed to conclude that finance ministry and FSLRC, in a hurry to resolve certain minor issues, ignored the evolution of the role of RBI and the care with which RBI has nurtured the financial sector. There are eminent analysts and economists who compare the role of RBI with that of Fed Reserve. The two central banks have two different histories and they function in two different worlds. To say that time is not right for dismantling or truncating the RBI which is doing creditably well as has been admitted in several international forums, would be telling the obvious.

The dissenting notes recorded by 4 out of 7 members who signed the final report of FSLRC are well-argued documents, which inter alia plead the case for maintaining the basic features of RBI and asserted the need for allowing the central bank to carry on with its present mandates. One wonders what motivated the FSLRC Chairman to finalize the report ignoring the difference of views expressed especially by K J Udeshi, P J Nayak and Y H Malegam.

It would appear that FSLRC was not adequately briefed about the relationship between the RBI and GOI. The regulatory apparatus plus legislations in financial sector in India are in working condition. It has to be admitted that till Dr. Rajan's emergence as an acceptable leader of the Indian financial sector, the FSLRC's effort to re-invent the institutional structure of regulatory bodies had pushed the regulators and supervisors with the exception of RBI to a confused state, making the possibility of an intelligent debate on the issue remote.

The idea of creating a Unified Financial Agency for all financial regulators except RBI, truncating RBI by separating Public Debt Management and keeping the agency doing that work (presumably with the same work force) in RBI premises, later UFA subsuming even RBI, all give a feeling that the FSLRC was not allowed to 'apply its intelligent mind' and in the eagerness to satisfy all, and so fast, it had forgotten its own original brief.

Perhaps, the purpose would be served better, if RBI is allowed to function with its present mandate, a coordination committee sorts out issues among the remaining regulators. If GOI aim is to reduce the number of regulators, after necessary groundwork, merger of the regulatory agencies outside RBI one by one, as work stabilizes could be thought of. The twin goals of one Unified Financial Agency and managing the manpower-related issues that may arise with merger here could be better handled this way.

*****

Monetary Policy Committee

This decade has seen Reserve Bank of India (RBI) emerging as a centre of attraction for almost all people, from Prime Minister Narendra Modi to the poorest citizen in PM's constituency Vaaraanasi. Earlier, common man had noted the Mahatma's smile on the notes issued by RBI and identified the central bank with one of its core functions, namely issue of currency. Two successive outspoken governors, Duvvuri Subbarao and Raghuram Rajan, in their own ways, have demystified Reserve Bank of India. Today RBI is understood in India, the way world understands it.

While Subbarao through his innovative financial inclusion initiatives took the message of RBI to every nook and corner of India, Rajan sent out a loud and clear message to the world that India's central bank has a functional team of professionals who can handle several dimensions of central banking functions simultaneously. These two governors took pains to study the evolution of RBI, originally conceived as an institution which would perform the functions similar to those the then Bank of England was handling in Britain, into an organization participating in every aspect of economic development, besides managing its core central banking functions like regulatory and supervisory roles in the financial sector together with currency management.

Like Tatas once used to say, "There is some steel in everybody's life," today every citizen's fortune is linked to policies pursued by the Reserve Bank of India.

Monetary Policy Committee

Contrary to the expectations of ordinary humans like this writer who criticized the attempt by the Financial Sector Legislative Reforms Commission (FSLRC) for writing a monologue report on dotted lines to satisfy certain vested interests, brushing aside all dissents even from within the Commission, we now find that the FSLRC report is being used as just a reference point for initiating long overdue reforms in the financial sector. The whole credit for this change of mindset in the finance ministry should go to one individual namely Dr. Raghuram G Rajan, who appeared on the scene at the right time and like an *avatar,* disappeared from the scene after almost completing his mission in about three years.

It is worthwhile to recall S S Tarapore's May 2013 observations on FSLRC: "The Commission recommends the setting up of a statutory Monetary Policy Committee (MPC) to take executive decisions on monetary policy with each member having a vote and the Chairperson having a veto, which must be explained with a public statement. The devil is in the detail.

There would be only two RBI members and five external members appointed by the Government. The Ministry of Finance nominee would be a non-voting member on the MPC but would articulate the Government viewpoint. With Big Brother watching over their shoulder, brave would be the external member who would deviate from the Government line. The RBI would be better off with the present arrangement.

The leitmotif of the FSLRC is to charge the gate of the temple of money with iconoclastic fervor. One prays that in this internecine battle, RBI's Pretorian Guards fight off the charge of the Commissioners. One must remember that countries that destroy their central banks destroy themselves."

Tarapore retired as Deputy Governor, RBI some twenty years ago. But post-retirement, literally till his last breath, he remained a watchdog of the rights and responsibilities of the central bank which he served for more than three decades. His writings and speeches during the last two decades can easily be prescribed as a treasure of teachings on policy formulation and implementation by RBI.

It is unfortunate that Tarapore did not live to see the changes that RBI under the able leadership of Dr. Rajan could bring about in the concept of MPC. In effect, while the RBI Governor is now unburdened of the individual responsibility of deciding on Monetary Policy, the central bank could get the existing arrangement of Technical Advisory Committee legalized and professionalized.

The six-member Monetary Policy Committee, constituted under the new dispensation during the last week of September 2016, has three renowned economists (Chetan Ghate from Indian Statistical Institute, Pami Dua from Delhi School of Economics and Ravindra Dholakia from IIM – Ahmedabad) nominated by GOI, the Deputy Governor (R Gandhi) and the Executive Director (Michael Patra) in charge of the concerned department in RBI as members with RBI Governor as Chairperson. In case of a tie, Governor will have a casting vote.

There is a conscious effort on the part of government to broad-base decision making and infuse professionalism in processes, as is evident from the accommodative approach to RBI's views on MPC and choice of government nominees from among the best available experts in the field.

The newly constituted MPC, going by the profiles of its 6 members is a professional body of experts, each member capable of applying his/her mind while participating in deliberations. RBI is known for allowing free expression of views in In-house meetings. During the Technical Advisory Committee days, though the final call was to be taken by the Governor, he benefit of individual perceptions expressed by the TAC members had helped decision-making to a great extent. Since the time the constitution of MPC was announced, a section of analysts has been apprehensive of MPC dividing itself into Team A (RBI) and Team B (GOI) and voting for constituency interests, making casting vote by Governor essential to take decisions. This uncharitable lament brings disgrace to the professional integrity of individual members.

We need to give a fair chance to MPC to evolve itself as an expert body unburdening the RBI Governor from individual responsibility for every policy decision.

Dr. Rajan during his tenure as Governor felt that, for all the unpalatable monetary policy decisions taken by the RBI by virtue of its position, the Government, the Finance Ministry, the Industrialists, Public Sector banks, and common man, affected by the decision were critical of RBI. The Governor had to bear the brunt of the attack as though he had done great injustice for his personal gains. Such a perception might have worked in favour of his support for a formal committee approach to decision-making, more than the half-baked recommendations on the subject by FSLRC.

In a way, MPC formalizes and professionalizes the existing Technical Advisory Committee (TAC) which has been advising RBI Governor on crucial issues concerning monetary policy. To the extent that TAC's advice was made known to the public, RBI has been trying to be transparent even where Governor differed from the TAC's perceptions. The present arrangement unburdens RBI Governor from individual responsibility in decisions on monetary policy and makes the MPC comprising experts more relevant.

The initial criticism that the Monetary Policy Committee suffers from imbalance of expertise as majority members happen to be professional economists should now fade out. While all the three GOI nominees are renowned economists, Governor, a Deputy Governor and an Executive Director from within RBI (one a career central banker and another a career economist, both with decades of relevant central banking and administrative experience) will be able to provide inputs on needs and expectations of banking sector and the economy in general.

In sum, the constitution of MPC strengthens RBI Governor's hands and sends out a clear signal that GOI is serious about retaining RBI's status as an expert professional body. The MPC met for the first time on the eve of October 4, 2016 Monetary

Policy Announcement which saw a base rate cut of 25 basis points. The decision by the MPC, reportedly, was unanimous. We need not read much into the unanimity in the MPC about the first rate cut. Such bodies have different ways of functioning, depending on the leadership provided by the Chairperson.

In this case, the harmless observation one can make is, after the deliberations, each one of the individual members would have decided to fall in line with the idea of going for a rate cut. Other than their own perceptions about the path inflation may take, the need to send out a message that the Committee will not remain satisfied with 'status quo' and is willing to move forward and experiment and the likely advancement of Union Budget presentation by a month would also have weighed in favour of the decision.

Inflation Targeting

Having appreciated the introduction of the concept of Committee approach to decision-making, let us not ignore the changes in policy formulation and implementation it signifies. In sum, while chasing the inflation target is the responsibility of Reserve Bank of India, the central bank has lost control of the major weapon in its armory for fighting inflation. The reference here is to the transfer of responsibility to decide policy rates to MPC.

It was in this context that while negotiating under the able leadership of Dr. Rajan, RBI accepted a flexible and moving inflation target (4 plus or minus 2 per cent with different milestones to be achieved at different points of time). Non-achievement of inflation target will have to be explained by RBI. Here what will matter is the way in which RBI articulates its views on the need to align fiscal and monetary policies to ensure optimum or 'optimum possible' economic growth, retaining the inflation within the targeted levels. The new RBI Governor Urjit Patel may not speak as often on these issues as his predecessor did, but is known for clarity of his perceptions.

Patel spoke much less in his maiden policy conference on October 4, but did not fail to put the records straight on RBI's stance on inflation targeting and clearly spell out his perceptions on future course. He referred to the pursuit of self-imposed targets and framework agreement with the government which preceded the amendments to the Reserve Bank of India Act and the associated notification. He further clarified that now all those ad hoc measures are superseded by the legal amendments and the notifications on constitution of MPC and setting out the inflation target at 4 per cent by 2021 with a 2 per cent tolerance level.

There has been some criticism in the media about the change in format of the Monetary Policy Statement issued after October 4, 2016 review. Some analysts tried to read inconsistency in the mention about upside risk of inflation and rate cut, forgetting that the rate cut was in 'present tense' and the possibility of upside risk was in future, to control which measures outside monetary policy, which have more to do with fiscal policy were also necessary.

Impact of Rate Cuts on Lending/Deposit Rates

While talking on rate cuts, one thing the previous RBI governor Raghuram Rajan was sadly aware all through his tenure was the slow trickling down of the impact of base rate reduction to the ultimate retail lending rates of banks, while he noticed quick action by banks in reducing deposit rates immediately following each rate cut. It is comforting to find that there is continuity of thought process in RBI on this aspect also. RBI Governor had this to say on the day of monetary Policy Announcement:

"I agree that the transmission through bank loans is less than any one of us would have liked. We are hoping that over the next quarter or two, keeping in mind that the government has also reduced small savings rate, the MCLR calculation will throw up more transmission. The transmission in new lending has been much better."

ICICI Bank reduced deposit rates by 15 to 25 basis points about a month prior to the October 4, 2016 rate cut by RBI. GOI, in the name of linking small savings rates to the yield on G Sec, nowadays reduce interests on small savings scheme instruments including PPF off and on. In his observation quoted earlier, RBI Governor was referring to the latest such reduction for the October-December 2016 quarter. The reduction was by 10 basis points (100 basis points = one percentage point). Perhaps, GOI may have to introduce differential interest rates, from a pure social security angle, offering interest at a percentage point higher for savers who are solely dependent on interest income for survival.

*****

Convergence of Fiscal and Monetary Policies

During the fortnight ended February 10, 2017, three documents which should give a fair idea to the common man about the Government of India's (GOI) approach to the management of the country's resources during the subsequent fiscal year (2017–18) and the Reserve Bank of India's (RBI) perception of the health of India's financial sector, post-demonetization, were released. These were The Economic Survey 2016–17, Union Budget 2017–18 and the Monetary Policy Statement released by RBI on February 8, 2017.

Economic Survey 2016–17

Traditionally, in India, Economic Survey is a document taking stock of the impact of government's policies and budgetary interventions on the growth profile of the economy and GOI's perceptions about the future growth trajectory, presented just before the presentation of central budget which serves as a guide for deliberations on the budget inside and outside parliament. Recent years have seen a healthy change in the drafting of Economic Survey with an untold agenda to use it as a tool for driving in new ideas, which are at a nascent stage, but if successfully 'marketed' can bring about faster changes in the economy and social sector.

This effort spearheaded by the Chief Economic Advisor Arvind Subramanian is more evident in the Economic Survey 2016–17 which has adopted a 'thematic' approach to issues covered by the Survey. We will touch upon two aspects here which can have a long term impact on the financial health of the country and the implementation of social sector schemes in the country. These relate to impact of demonetization on RBI's balance sheet and introduction of the concept of Universal Basic Income (UBI).

Demonetization Bonanza?

The Economic Survey 2016–17 observes:

"Meanwhile, some amount of unreturned high denomination notes. The December 30, 2016 Ordinance has declared the unreturned notes as no longer constituting legal tender. When the grace period expires, the RBI could declare that these unreturned notes are no longer valid in any way, either as legal tender or as assets that can be exchanged for new currency. When this occurs, the associated liability will be extinguished, and the RBI's net worth will increase. In this sense, demonetization has effected a transfer of wealth from holders of illicit black money to the public sector, which can then be redeployed in various productive ways – to retire government debt, recapitalize banks, or even redistribute back to the private sector."

The idea cannot be faulted on theory. But the flip side is, the arguments are built up in isolation and by drawing comparisons with small and big nations elsewhere whose stage of development, pattern of governance, role expectations from central banks and relationship between central bank and the exchequer are no way comparable with the role expectations from RBI. For instance the Reserve Balances with Federal Reserve System as on February 8, 2017 was over $2.2 trillion (public debt about $14 trillion). RBI's share capital and reserves worked out to about $35 billion (India's public debt $850 billion). Moreover, as recently observed by former RBI Governor Dr. Y V Reddy, the interdependence of monetary and fiscal policies in the Indian context makes reading of RBI Balance Sheet in isolation meaningless. Of course, Reddy didn't tell it so bluntly. He said, government's finances and RBI's resources are interrelated.

This is a wider issue and here only some preliminary observations are made, by way of caution against any hurried action in the context of arguments put forth in the Economic Surveys 2015–16 and 2016–17 for sucking out capital and reserves of RBI for redeployment in sectors normally financed from GOI's resources.

Universal Basic Income (UBI)

Prefixed by a couple of excellent memorable quotes from Mahatma Gandhi, Chapter 9 of Economic Survey introduces Universal basic Income asunder:

"Wiping every tear from every eye" based on the principles of universality, unconditionality, and agency—the hallmarks of a Universal Basic Income (UBI)—is a conceptually appealing idea. A number of implementation challenges lie ahead, especially the risk that UBI would become an add-on to, rather than a replacement of, current anti-poverty and social programs, which would make it fiscally unaffordable. But given their multiplicity, costs, and questionable effectiveness, and the real opportunities afforded by the rapidly improving "JAM" infrastructure, UBI holds the prospects of improving upon the status quo. This chapter provides some illustrative costs for a UBI (varying between 4 percent and 5 percent of GDP), and outlines a number of ideas to take UBI forward, highlighting the practical difficulties. UBI's appeal to both ends of the political spectrum makes it an idea whose time has come perhaps not for immediate implementation but at least for serious public deliberation. The Mahatma would have been conflicted by the idea but, on balance, might have endorsed it.

So far, discussions on such issues were isolated or confined to academia or research efforts.

For India, once the political leadership gets convinced about a realistic UBI, resources will not be a problem. One possibility is, some vested interests will hijack the proposal of UBI to mix it with "unemployment dole," an unhealthy practice existing in developed countries. While this should be avoided, care should also be taken to ensure that where employment assurance schemes are implemented, the compensations should be realistic.

There are several pockets in India, including many in states like Kerala, where the local population has successfully eliminated poverty and come up with regard to crucial human development indicators. Attribute it to militant trade unionism or the colour of the flags held by parties in power, the credit for this goes to the insistence by workers for a minimum basic wage.

Hopefully the concept of Universal Basic Minimum Income, as the debate picks up, will result in healthy deliberations on the need for grassroots level improvements in income distribution to ensure sustainable economic growth. A pragmatic approach to the sharing of wealth can reduce several security concerns world over and ensure better living conditions, not only for the deprived class, but for many from the rich and the powerful who feel insecure today.

It may be recalled that the Seventh Central Pay Commission (CPC) had fixed the minimum wage for central government employees at Rs. 18,000.

Viewed in the above context, GOI will have to concede at some stage the demand for some reasonable relativity for wages of the workers in the unorganised sector with the entitlements of workers in the organized sector having comparable responsibilities. Whenever specific issues relating to job security and compensation are raised by unions or external agencies in the context of human development indicators in India showing uncomfortably low levels in comparison with similarly placed developing countries, some sporadic initiatives are taken by Centre or state governments.

One such initiative is the introduction of the concept of 'full-benefit fixed-term jobs' in the labour-intensive garment sector by the Narendra Modi government recently. However, a comprehensive legislation covering all aspects of service in the unorganised sector is not yet thought of.

Time is opportune to revisit the prices, wages and income policy. If we do not do this, labour migration issues within the country and flight of skills and expertise from India may rise to unmanageable levels giving rise to several social problems. The revamp of prices, wages and income policy need to be done quickly and for making the processes transparent and findings and subsequent action plans acceptable for the stakeholders, there should be meaningful debates in legislatures and with users of services of workers.

Strikes like the one on 2 September 2016 should be seen as symptoms of growing labour unrest should be an 'eye opener' for initiating corrective action. Protests like this should not be evaluated based on success and failure or losses and gains. Simmering discontent in the workforce emanating from the feeling that there is exploitation by the users of services, taking advantage of the helplessness of the workers, affect productivity and can have long term negative impact on economic growth. Sooner the governments and corporates amend the present approach, the better for the country. Mentioned this to draw attention to the need for ensuring distributive justice in compensations which by itself will reduce the need for subventions of several categories to meet social security needs.

Monetary Policy Stance

The Monetary Policy Statement presented by RBI Governor Urjit Patel on February 8, 2017 made the following statement:

"The large overhang of liquidity consequent upon demonetization weighed on money markets in

December, but from mid-January rebalancing has been underway with expansion of currency in circulation and new bank notes being injected into the system at an accelerated pace. Throughout this period, the Reserve Bank's market operations have been in liquidity absorption mode. With the abolition of the incremental cash reserve ratio from December 10, liquidity management operations have consisted of variable rate reverse repos under the LAF of tenors ranging from overnight to 91 days and auctions of cash management bills under the market stabilisation scheme (MSS) of tenors ranging from 14 to 63 days. The average daily net absorption under the LAF was 1.6 trillion in December, 2.0 trillion in January and 3.7 trillion in February (upto February 7) while under the MSS, it was 3.8 trillion, 5.0 trillion and 2.9 trillion, respectively. Money market rates remained aligned with the policy repo rate albeit with a soft bias, with the weighted average call money rate (WACR) averaging 18 basis points below the policy rate during December and January."

Analyses and articles appearing in the mainstream media these days, in a routine manner, gives an impression that central bank's monetary policy hovers around upward or downward revision of base rates alone. It is common knowledge now that post – November 8, 2016, there has been deposit growth in banks to the extent that banks were finding it difficult to deploy their resources in remunerative avenues. Mentioned this because, this time around, any change in RBI's base rates would not have had much impact on the pool of resources of banks and therefore, one need not be concerned too much about the central bank having left the base rates untouched for the present.

Fiscal Responsibility and Budget Management (FRBM)

The N K Singh Committee which reviewed Fiscal Responsibility and Budget Management (FRBM) Act has submitted its report to the finance ministry. The highlights of the committee's recommendations reported in the media include:

- Space for government to spend more on development (translated into common man's language, this would mean rise in government borrowings),
- A slightly higher fiscal deficit target (perhaps a band of 3 to 3.5 per cent of GDP in place of the present target of 3 per cent of GDP for FY18 (Keeping in view the leeway to spend more in 2017–18, Chief Economic Advisor is reported to have expressed his dissent on a rigid target)
- Panel members were of the view that the report should be made public only after Budget 2017–18

Differences of views among various stakeholders notwithstanding, no wonder that the arithmetic of Budget 2017–18 got impacted by the four-volume report.

The Budget Speech takes note of the N K Singh Committee report and observes asunder:

"The FRBM Review Committee has given its report recently. The Committee has done an elaborate exercise and has recommended that a sustainable debt path must be the principal macro-economic anchor of our fiscal policy. The Committee has favoured Debt to GDP of 60% for the General Government by 2023, consisting of 40% for Central Government and 20% for State Governments. Within this framework, the Committee has derived and recommended 3% fiscal deficit for the next three years. The Committee has also provided for 'Escape Clauses,' for deviations upto 0.5% of GDP, from the stipulated fiscal deficit target. Among the triggers for taking recourse to these Escape Clauses, the Committee has included "far-reaching structural reforms in the economy with unanticipated fiscal implications" as one of the factors. Although there is a strong case now to invoke this Escape Clause, I am refraining from doing so. The Report of the Committee will be carefully examined and appropriate decisions taken in due course."

Conflict Between Fiscal and Monetary Policies?

Reserve Bank of India Governor Urjit Patel who is a member of the Review Panel, speaking at the Vibrant Gujarat Summit on January 11, 2017, made the following observations:

"While some government guarantees and limited subventions can help, steep interest rate subventions and large credit guarantees also impede optimal allocation of financial resources and increases moral hazard. The mandates for these have to be narrow, and thus perforce be deployed judiciously, within a regulatory framework, which RBI has suggested. Guarantees increase government's contingent liabilities, and add to risk premia for its own borrowing.

Guarantees per se at the end of the day have limited utility in solving important sector issues. For example, for small scale enterprises, perhaps non – pecuniary and transaction costs related to clearances, inspections and the taxation bureaucracy are more important our general government deficit (that is borrowing by the centre and states combined) is, according to IMF data, amongst the highest in the group of G-20 countries. In conjunction, the level of our general government debt as a ratio to GDP is cited by some as coming in the way of a credit rating upgrade. We have to take cognisance of these comparisons and facts as we go forward to make progress. Specifically, this will help us to better manage risks for ourselves, and thereby mitigate financial volatility. In the context of an already adverse external environment that I mentioned earlier, this assumes more importance.

Borrowing even more and pre-empting resources from future generations by governments cannot be a short cut to long-lasting higher growth. Instead, structural reforms and reorienting government expenditure towards public infrastructure are key for durable gains on the Indian growth front."

These observations of Urjit Patel coming at this juncture gains significance because a supportive fiscal policy is imperative for RBI in chasing the now 'mandatory' Inflation Target of 4 per cent (plus or minus 2 per cent with certain pre-decided milestones).

Though for the outside world and media the differences of views between GOI and RBI provide entertainment stuff, all along, the two (GOI and RBI) have saved the marriage between fiscal and monetary policies by appropriate 'give and take' and an unwritten understanding that 'divorce' is not an option.

Government Borrowings and Interest Rates

US has a per capita public debt of $65,000 (Total outstanding debt touching $20 trillion!). But that country gets government bonds subscribed not just by 'public,' but by outside world also. In India, public debt really gets subscribed by public, using the captive catchment area of SLR and funds of public sector organisations like LIC. Thus, till such time government securities really become market-friendly, whatever be the arguments in favour of increased borrowing, GOI will have to exercise caution. For the reasons stated here, as the funds mobilized by banks and financial institutions are dictated by market forces, GOI does not have much maneuverability on costs of borrowings.

Challenging Job for CEA and RBI

The Economic Survey and the Budget 2017–18 presented on February 1, 2017 gave more credence to the impression that it was going to be a tight rope walk for GOI and RBI to balance the fiscal and monetary policy compulsions from getting exposed to the influence of distrust which was slowly building up in the minds of savers of funds and users of resources for various political and policy reasons in recent months. India's economic growth will not depend on the prophecies of economists and analysts, but on how Urjit Patel and Arun Jaitley handle the conflicting interests of monetary and fiscal policies during the coming years.

*****

SECTION II

Note-Ban and After

Mainstreaming Cash Flows

Though I am not one of those who follow the impact of planetary positions on individuals' and nations' destinies or consult an astrologer when something goes wrong or when I initiate something auspicious, circumstances lead me to think that the current decade is a lucky period for India as a nation. From somewhere leaders emerge and change the way we look at things, giving deeper insight into what is better for the country. While one can remember several names, those of Arvind Kejriwal, Narendra Modi and Raghuram Rajan remain uppermost in one's mind. First two for creating an awareness about rampant corruption across sectors and political ideologies and Dr. Rajan for exposing the link between erosion of nation's wealth and management of financial sector.

In India, corruption in high places has been recognized as a roadblock to economic growth and distributive justice, by a strange coincidence, almost concurrently with the emergence of economic reforms, liberalization and globalization, circa 1990's. I would attribute the transformation of the Indian political scene in Modi's favour, to the India Against Corruption movement, and Modi's decisive electoral victory to the confidence he could instill in people, about his ability to take a diversion from the status quo and engage directly with the 'stakeholders' of corruption irrespective of their positions and political affiliations. Modi's election promises on handling black money and corruption got converted into votes in NDA's favour in 2014 elections.

The leadership provided by Modi enabled the NDA government to initiate action to bring transparency in transactions and plug the holes in porous financial management practices followed by government. The Reserve Bank of India and several ministries in GOI were already aware of the need to revamp the institutional system in the financial sector and reorientation of policies to suit the changes that had already taken place in the business environment world over. The several measures initiated by RBI to introduce new players in the financial system and a thorough health check up of the loan portfolios of major banks, the GOI focus on strengthening public sector banks and financial inclusion need to be seen in this perspective. Demonetisation of high denomination currencies is a continuation of the measures to mainstream monetary transactions through legal channels.

Demonetisation of Rs. 1000 and Rs. 500 Notes

As it is primarily a Government of India decision to demonetize highest value currency notes of Rs. 500 and Rs. 1000, we can safely rely on the background explained by the Prime Minister while announcing the strong and decisive step on November 8, 2016. After referring briefly his government's resolve to fight the challenges posed by terrorism, corruption and black money, PM listed the major initiatives taken since NDA came to power, which included (a) the law passed in 2015 for disclosure of foreign black money;

(b) agreements with many countries including the US, to add provisions for sharing banking information; (c) the strict law to curb *benami* transactions, which are used to deploy black money earned through corruption and (d) the scheme introduced for declaring black money after paying a stiff penalty. PM mentioned that these measures have so far brought into the open nearly Rs. 1,25,000 crore rupees of black money belonging to the corrupt.

Prime Minister announced the decision that "the Rs. 500 and Rs. 1000 currency notes, presently in use, will no longer be legal tender from midnight tonight, that is November 8, 2016." He qualified this step as a continuation of earlier measures to break the grip of corruption and black money and said that the step will strengthen the hands of the common man in the fight against corruption, black money and fake currency. After explaining the procedural formalities and timeframe for deposit/exchange of notes which are no more legal tender, PM concluded his speech admitting possibility of temporary hardships to citizens and exhorting all to join the 'festival of integrity and credibility.

As the measure had an impact on the lives of all, response from the media and analysts has been cautious and 'measured.' Though most of the people refrained from questioning the necessity of the step, as nobody wanted to be seen themselves as advocates of the corrupt and hoarders of black money, many raised objection to the lack of preparation for implementing such a large scale operation. It has to be said to the credit of bank employees that within the constraints, the implementation of the measure was handled efficiently.

Objectives of Demonetization

Motives behind the move which has been variously described as 'Surgical Strike' and 'shock therapy' has been well articulated in Prime Minister Modi's speech announcing demonetization. I am not joining the hazardous game of making further guesses which many in the electronic, print and social media are already at, as part of their 'regular job.' Common man would console himself that all the pain was not in vain, even if the measure partially succeeds in 'purifying' the economy and checking growth of corruption. The mainstreaming of idle currency will bring a large amount of 'hidden' wealth into books of accounts and that definitely have not only positive tax implications, but will be a deterrent to further accumulation of wealth from ugly sources. Compulsion to do more transactions through banking channels will be a disincentive for further 'import' or local printing of counterfeit currency.

Future Course

The mainstreaming of 'idle currency' will have to be quickly followed up with measures like regulating transactions in gold and property by making mandatory provisions to route them through banks and sooner the political leadership (as different from the government) comes to a consensus on such measures, the better for the country.

A couple of issues, which even analysts of repute avoid mentioning, may be for fear of becoming unpopular, but will have long term beneficial impact for the country's economic growth and India's image among developing/developed nations, remain still in the backburner. They are handling the taxation of agricultural income and mapping the assets including gold and jewelry lying unaccounted in various pockets. Government could start with making it mandatory to report periodically the value of assets above a pre-decided threshold level, held by individuals and registered institutions.

Some Afterthoughts

In the whole process of implementation of demonetization of Rs. 500 and Rs. 1000 notes, government and banking system (including the regulator) missed a couple of steps they could have taken much earlier to November 8, 2016, the date on which the demonetization was announced, had the system applied its mind. These steps relate to readying at least majority of ATMs for dispensing the new design high denomination notes, print order for which had been given long back and stocking low denomination currency in semi-urban and rural areas where people were still using more hard cash than ATMs or electronic payment systems for their day to day money transactions. In hindsight, this could have been managed without affecting the 'secrecy' needed to be maintained while making the announcement.

Till recently, banking did not make its physical presence in India, much beyond 'walkable' distance from points where a four-wheeler can reach. It didn't make much difference when ATMs took over the work of cash dispensation from banks, as ATMs crowded cities and towns and Public Sector Banks which were forced to go to rural areas and open branches or service rural clientele too, went by and large by the 'walkable' distance rule. Those who are responsible for this state of affairs are enjoying the fun of being in the opposition now. The imported concepts of Banking Correspondents is yet to take roots in India. An RBI Governor (Dr. Raghuram Rajan) who understood the problems and initiated some revolutionary reforms in the financial sector including the concept of small banks and as using Post Offices as conduits for banking services to improve outreach was eased out fast.

As the idea of phasing out Rs. 500 and Rs. 1000 notes were somewhere in the back of the mind of policy makers, even while print order for Rs. 2000 notes were being given and instructions were being issued for increasing supply of lower value notes for circulation, without affecting the secrecy of demonetization announcement, simultaneous measures should have been taken to:

a) Prepare at least fifty per cent of the ATMs ready for dispensing new high denomination notes of different dimensions and
b) Suck out Rs. 500 and Rs. 1000 notes from rural areas which could have been done in the guise of poor people who were really having problems in handling high denomination currency. Many of them were dependent on daily wages which were less than Rs. 500!

One possible reason for the chaotic position is outsourcing of work by institutions in piece-meal to agencies which have no moral allegiance to the institutions which hire them. We need to invent new strategies to build up reliable relationships between masters and servants, in the modern era of hiring and firing at higher levels and contract/bonded labour at lower levels.

*****

A God-sent Opportunity to Cleanse the System

Opportunity to govern a country, like life, comes sans 'rewind' and 'fast forward' buttons. Prime Minister Narendra Modi's case is no exception. Without going astray in a philosophical mood, let me straight come to the point. Right or wrong, Modi has no option to go back on the announcement of November 8, 2016 withdrawing the 'legal tender' status of high value notes (Rs. 500 and Rs. 1000). The only option now before government and the nation is to implement what is now called in general parlor as 'demonetization' with least pain to the people and ensure that the country is benefited by achieving the purpose clearly mentioned while announcing the decision namely, 'fighting black money and terrorism and minimizing presence of fake currency in the system.'

Unintended Consequences

Former Prime Minister Manmohan Singh concluding his article "Making of a mammoth tragedy" in The Hindu on December 9, 2016 observed asunder:

'Black money is a menace to our society that we need to eliminate. In doing so, we have to be mindful of the potential impact on hundreds of millions of other honest citizens. It may be tempting and self-fulfilling to believe that one has all the solutions and previous governments were merely lackadaisical in their attempts to curb black money. It is not so. Leaders and governments have to care for their weak and at no point can they abdicate their responsibility. Most policy decisions carry risks of unintended consequences. It is important to deftly balance these risks with the potential benefits of such decisions. Waging a war on black money may sound enticing. But it cannot entail even a single loss of life of an honest Indian.'

Conceding his right to be concerned, let us also remember, all martyrs were honest citizens. The arguments put forth only explains the rationale behind his reluctance to take decisions during the ten year period when Manmohan Singh was Prime Minister. Manmohan Singh's brief, but forthright indictment of demonetization in Parliament was more explicit. Though the harsh language seemed having been smuggled into the speech by his sponsors, by and large the outburst represented his resentment with the management of economy and financial sector in India for decades now, simmering in his mind.

The managers of the Indian Economy and the Indian Financial Sector, who opted to procrastinate action against the looting of the common man in India post-liberalisation should pro rata share the entire blame contained in the Manmohan Singh's 6 minutes speech and his laments quoted above. Generations to come will remember MMS for this speech, as it is not a political speech, but one backed by long years of experience as economist of international repute, central banker, finance minister and Prime Minister.

Dr. Manmohan Singh's advice to 'reflect' on the content of his speech needs to be taken seriously by all including the victims (common man) and factored in, in their future action plans. Instead of throwing the ball back, alleging that MMS did not act or speak at appropriate times or in appropriate forums, policy makers should opt to commission the former PM's experience and wisdom to make midway corrections in the crusade against corruption, fake currency and terrorism. Once he cools down, definitely he will help and never leave you in the lurch. After all, having managed an unwieldy coalition for a long time, more than anyone else, Dr. Manmohan Singh is aware of the constraints with which governments work.

Manmohan Singh is not alone. Bloomberg published a story filed by Vrishti Beniwal & Anirban Nag captioned "Central banker missing in action as India escalates war on cash" referring to the low key participation of RBI in managing the post-demonetization problems in banks. Following closely on the heels of a BBC lament about how India will handle 20 billion pieces of useless currency notes, Bloomberg story was interesting reading, indeed. Let us not underplay the anxieties of external agencies, though they have only pedestrian interest in India's real problems. Let us have a look:

First, RBI Governor has spoken just only once, since November 8 announcement of demonetization. Earlier, someone had researched and found out that during the entire 2 years plus tenure as Deputy Governor, Urjit Patel had made only one public speech against the tally of fifty-plus, posted by one of his colleagues and two dozen posted by his immediate predecessor Dr. Raghuram Rajan.

To put records straight RBI Governor did speak to media more than a couple of occasions and clarified the central bank's position on currency management and problems faced by banking sector. Of course, the leadership team in RBI met the press formally after the monetary policy announcement on December 7.

Two, the observation "a senior bureaucrat was tasked with firefighting" is based on a senior Secretary in the Finance Ministry explaining the measures taken by GOI to ameliorate the inconvenience caused by withdrawal of the legal tender character of Rs. 500 and Rs. 1000 notes announced by PM on November 8. In the given context the official was doing his assigned duty, while RBI was busy with 'follow up' measures. Robert Hocket, who talks in 'general' terms, appears to be totally out of touch with the Indian context.

Three, K C Chakrabarty, another person whom the writers have contacted, has already gone on record saying that when he was RBI Deputy Governor, the demonetization proposal received in RBI (he said it was immaterial whether the proposal was made over the phone or in writing) to which, in his words, "We said, no." So the 'benefit of doubt' offered by him to Urjit Patel must be genuine.

Four, though repeated references are being made to 1978 demonetization in the media by analysts, the context, content and magnitude of the 2016 measure make any such comparison ridiculous.

Did Anything Go Wrong?

It is always easy to be wiser after the event. Let us not brush aside the criticism against inadequate preparations made before demonetization of Rs. 1000 and Rs. 500 notes announced by Prime Minister Narendra Modi on November 8, 2016 or for that matter the gravity of the sufferings the measure inflicted upon unsuspecting innocent elders and poor people in remote villages of India. It is, in a way, comforting to see that, media and vigilant social activists are making work easier for those who do post mortem, audit, post-project analyses of project implementation, inspections, various judicial processes and enquiries/investigations by recording evidence on an ongoing basis.

The November 8, 2016 Announcement

What one understands from Prime Minister Narendra Modi's November 8 speech announcing that high denomination currency note of value Rs. 500 and Rs. 1000 will not be legal tender from the midnight of Tuesday, November 2016 is that the action is in exercise of GOI's power to alter the legal tender character of currency notes.

The GOI announcement does not impact the RBI's promise to pay 'value' or the sovereign guarantee printed on the currency note. Therefore, legally, it would be wrong to make any adjustment in Reserve bank of India's balance sheet with reference to the quantum of notes surrendered within any stipulated time limit. Such adhocism in accounting practices can lead to erosion of trust in institutions like Reserve bank of India.

The misconception which got circulated through media, though in a small circle, that it would be perfectly legal to accept old Rs. 500 and Rs. 1000 notes in the normal course of transactions till December 30, 2016 or March 31, 2017 (As RBI will be exchanging these notes till that date) has since been removed. Extended time limits allowed for certain essential services like Railways, petrol outlets, hospitals etc relate to accountable transactions and these entities will be able to show source of further accumulation of high value notes after the midnight of November 8, 2016.

The Measure Has Been Accepted, by and Large

By and large, national and international media and monetary institutions have accepted the rationale behind the demonetization. While some were cautious in their appreciation, New York Times quoted an expert saying it was a wise move and went on to observe in an article: "The plan, top secret until Mr. Modi's announcement, was hailed by financial analysts as bold and potentially transformational for India. It is also a high-stakes experiment."

RBI Restoring Trust

Dr. Raghuram G. Rajan, then Governor RBI, on September 3rd 2016, at St. Stephen's College, New Delhi commenced his speech with the following observations:

"Over the last few weeks, I have outlined the RBI's approach to inflation, distressed debt, financial inclusion, banking sector reform, and market reform. Today,

I'd like to first discuss why central banking is not as easy as it appears (just raise or cut interest rates!) and why it needs decisions, sometimes unpopular or hard-to-explain ones, to be made under conditions of extreme uncertainty. This will then lead in to my arguments about why we need an independent central bank."

Rajan's efforts to preserve India's central bank in one piece did yield dividends. Reserve Bank of India managed the multi-dimensional threats to the financial system posed by the side-effects of demonetization within the constraints RBI and GOI are working today. The quick absorption of excess liquidity in the system by using the instrument of CRR, fast responses to changing needs in the supply of currency and above all the assurance that the interests of genuine depositors and borrowers are safe need to be seen in this context.

As always, RBI through its monetary policy announcement on December 7, 2016 has once again proved that its decisions are based on its own perceptions and not influenced by media lobbying or other external influences. India could sail through several tough economic crises in the past, only because monetary policy interventions and other measures by the central bank unreservedly supported government policy.

On August 29, 2013, Dr. Duvvuri Subbarao concluded his Swan Song on the eve of completion of a tumultuous five year term as RBI Governor with the following observation:

There has been a lot of media coverage on policy differences between the government and the Reserve Bank. Gerard Schroeder, the former German

Chancellor, once said, "I am often frustrated by the the Bundesbank. But thank God, it exists." I do hope Finance Minister Chidambaram will one day say, "I am often frustrated by the Reserve Bank, so frustrated that I want to go for a walk, even if I have to walk alone. But thank God, the Reserve Bank exists."

Subbarao's successor Dr. Raghuram Rajan brought more transparency in the working of RBI and sorted out some relationship issues between GOI and RBI during the 3 year period 2013–16. The transition of Technical Advisory Committee which advised Governor on monetary policy into the present 'independent' Monetary Policy Committee, besides unburdening Governor from individual responsibility for all monetary policy decisions has infused more professionalism in RBI's decision making.

When there is lot of confusion in the air even about the motives of the November 8 announcement withdrawing the legal tender status of high value notes, RBI's coming out with the central bank's perceptions about currency management and related matters will go a long way in restoring people's trust in the banking system. The clarification given by Governor Urjit Patel that the measure by itself will not have an immediate impact on RBI Balance Sheet should set at rest the speculations about GOI having an eye on a windfall gain from 'demonetization.' In the business of banking, trust is of paramount significance.

The currency note of Rs. 2 and above carries a promise ("I promise to pay the bearer the sum of... rupees") signed by Reserve Bank of India governor and a sovereign guarantee ("Guaranteed by the

Central Government"). The promise and guarantee are not governed by any date line. Prime Minister Modi's November 8, 2016 announcement has talked only about the 'legal tender' character of Rs. 500 and Rs. 1000 notes and has not withdrawn the promise by RBI to pay value or the sovereign guarantee that accompanies the promise.

Deadlines for exchange/deposit of the affected notes can at best be construed as ones fixed for administrative convenience of implementation of the scheme. Making notional entries in RBI's books to create income by extinguishing liabilities against notes 'withdrawn from circulation' and not reaching back RBI, within a stipulated deadline can have perilous long term implications.

Though so far the gossiping is only in the media, and no proposals have come from the GOI/RBI side, a couple of points need to go on record. There are outer contours up to which governments can play such games taking judiciary and people for granted. The sanctity of public trust need to be preserved at any cost and if governments allow to be guided or lured by possibility of short term gains, the negative impact on financial sector and economy can be a multiple of the notional temporary gains. If one needs an example, such measures will have immediate repercussions on public debt.

Ajay Shah in an article "A monetary economics view of the demonetization" in Business Standard (November 14), observed that "Money is the lubricant of the economy" which reminds one of a 'Times View/Counter View' column about corruption, some years back, where one side argued that 'corruption is the lubricant of the wheel of economic growth.' The article, by a deft theoretical approach, almost confused the reader to think that money is cash and reduced amount of money in circulation is, by itself, something bad for the economy.

The decision to demonetize presumes hoarding of high value currency for purposes other than normal genuine transactions, existence of fake currency in the system and evasion of tax by off-the-book high value transactions as in purchase of gold and property. Though there have been initial flip-flops, by and large, it appears, Reserve Bank of India has taken care to ensure availability of currency notes in exchange and for withdrawal from banks. Looks, there was a slip in making ATMs ready to dispense new Rs. 2000 and Rs. 500 notes.

Slowly the entire world is moving towards a cashless society (different from world without money!) and though India, with the present level of literacy and banking infrastructure, may not be able to keep pace with the developed world, cannot stand still, either.

As regards the success of demonetization now under way, common man would console himself that all the pain was not in vain, even if the measure partially succeeds in 'purifying' the economy and checking growth of corruption. The mainstreaming of idle currency will bring a large amount of 'hidden' wealth into books of accounts and that definitely have not only positive tax implications, but will be a deterrent to further accumulation of wealth from ugly sources. Compulsion to do more transactions through banking channels will be a disincentive for further 'import' or local printing of counterfeit currency.

Go Ahead Signal from C Rangarajan

Former RBI Governor C Rangarajan's article "Making the most of demonetization" in The Hindu Business Line (November 16) must give a lot of comfort to those who initiated action for 'Demonetization' and the thousands who are working 24x7 for implementing it as efficiently as possible with minimum pain for the common man, as the 'Go ahead' signal comes from an informed and unbiased veteran who has the backing of an entire life's experience in practical central banking with post-retirement association with policy making at the highest level in government.

Former RBI Governor has endorsed the three objectives of targeting black money in the form of currency, funding of terrorism through cash and making fake currency which found mention in PM's November 8, 2016 speech announcing demonetization, suggesting positive measures to achieve these objectives.

Taking the advice seriously, policy makers need to quicken the measures to prevent further accumulation of black money and to flush out the huge quantities of unaccounted wealth concealed in sectors like gold and jewelry, real estate and accounts abroad, leaving the burden of minimizing the pains caused mainly by planning and logistic problems to executives down the line with guidance from Reserve Bank of India.

The two steps suggested by Rangarajan in this context relating to keeping the tax rates at moderate levels and Electoral Reforms (though not specifically mentioned, government funding of electoral expenses based on need – the rich who fight election should not get this facility – is an immediate priority area) are significant and can go to the drawing board simultaneously with the preparation of Budget 2017–18.

Hardships are Real

The hardships experienced by the people of a country which is dependent on cash for several day-to-day transactions are real, though the long term benefits outweigh the temporary inconveniences. The link between corruption and black money and abuse of accumulated cash by miscreants had become unbreakable without some drastic measure of this magnitude.

There is need to simultaneously go vigorously on financial inclusion by activating and use Jan Dhan Yojana (JDY) accounts, timely prevention of use of channels like Railway ticket booking to bypass legal routes for exchange of old high value notes and disincentivize use of currency as a 'store of value' brought out in the article should draw the attention of the authorities for immediate follow-up action.

Tasks Ahead

When 'normal' banking business resumes, and it will, much faster than many of us think, there will be an attitudinal change not only on the side of the clientele, but for those responsible for formulation and implementation of banking policy and the human beings (we have found how far technology can serve you without the men behind the machines during these days!) converting the policy into action plans and the reaching out to the individual depositor/borrower. For a short period, banks need not have to worry about deposit mobilization and big borrowers are, hopefully, aware of the need to keep their assets 'performing,' so that banks are not forced to categorise their credit as NPAs. Banks should use this temporary respite provided through measures taken by GOI and RBI to put their houses in order. Banks can broad-base lending, improve their outreach to semi-urban and rural areas, increase their direct involvement in lending and supervision of MFIs with which they are associated and improve their image before the public.

If banks start providing credit liberally to small businesses especially in informal sector and GOI/RBI quickly sort out grass-root level issues arising from the sudden sterilization of the functioning of cooperatives (as in Kerala) and MFIs and NBFCs HFCs in most of the states by allowing them to handle old notes already accepted in repayment of loans and other genuine transactions below a reasonable cut off limit, the problems that have surfaced so far may not be insurmountable. It will be another matter, if the dissent is allowed to simmer and issues that need to be resolved by quick policy interventions are left to hairsplitting judicial scrutiny or to be allowed to be sorted out on the streets by masses who are aggrieved.

*****

Indian Banking System: Safe, Secure and Trustworthy

Reserve Bank of India Governor Urjit Patel in his brief and crisp 2017 New Year message to RBI family summed up his perception about the events during 2016 and the tasks ahead asunder:

"During the year gone by, we have continued our efforts at restoring macroeconomic stability in the economy. While the policy actions have already shown positive effects, nevertheless they are work in progress and need to be fine-tuned constantly to keep pace with the changing environment. Internally we continue to focus on enhancing specialization within the organization, even while strengthening the performance evaluation system to help identify areas requiring improvement and initiating appropriate skilling interventions. It is said that nothing is constant except change and we are in the midst of constantly changing times, throwing new challenges our way every day. I am confident that all of us working together will rise to the occasion and face these challenges in a manner befitting the reputation of this esteemed organization. Our recent engagement with withdrawal of SBNs is a case in point.

While on the subject, let me emphasize that one thing we should all zealously guard is the integrity and reputation of our organization and any act belittling the same should deserve zero tolerance from all of us. Needless to add, the Ban has achieved the present level of excellence only due to our collective efforts towards a common goal."

In his speech at the Vibrant Gujarat Investor Summit on January 11, 2017, RBI Governor, among other things, observed asunder:

"While some government guarantees and limited subventions can help, steep interest rate subventions and large credit guarantees also impede optimal allocation of financial resources and increases moral hazard. The mandates for these have to be narrow, and thus perforce be deployed judiciously, within a regulatory framework, which RBI has suggested. Guarantees increase government's contingent liabilities, and add to risk premia for its own borrowing. Guarantees per se at the end of the day have limited utility in solving important sector issues. For example, for small scale enterprises, perhaps non – pecuniary and transaction costs related to clearances, inspections and the taxation bureaucracy are more important our general government deficit (that is borrowing by the centre and states combined) is, according to IMF data, amongst the highest in the group of G-20 countries. In conjunction, the level of our general government debt as a ratio to GDP is cited by some as coming in the way of a credit rating upgrade. We have to take cognisance of these comparisons and facts as we go forward to make progress. Specifically, this will help us to better manage risks for ourselves, and thereby mitigate financial volatility. In the context of an already adverse external environment that I mentioned earlier, thisassumes more importance.

Borrowing even more and pre-empting resources from future generations by governments cannot be a short cut to long-lasting higher growth. Instead, structural reforms and reorienting government expenditure towards public infrastructure are key for durable gains on the Indian growth front."

Excerpts quoted above are only to draw attention to the short speech (accessible at rbi.org.in) which is a timely warning to policy makers in government against taking adverse long term decisions for short term gains. The takeaways in the RBI Governor's guidance include:

- Need to balance interest rate subventions and subsidies with real time benefits vis a vis other options to exhilarate economic growth,
- Not to look at long term government borrowings as a soft option, and
- Be mindful of criticism from international agencies so that creditworthiness of the nation is preserved.

Keeping the broad perspectives about the state of the economy and perceptions about the tasks ahead spelt out by Urjit Patel, let us have a look at the present status and future prospects of the Indian Financial Sector.

Monetary Policy

Monetary policy announced by RBI on December 7, 2016 made the following observations which have a bearing on banking business:

"Liquidity conditions have undergone large shifts in Q3 so far. Surplus conditions in October and early November were overwhelmed by the impact of the withdrawal of SBNs from November 9. Currency in circulation plunged by 7.4 trillion up to December 2; consequently, net of replacements, deposits surged into the banking system, leading to a massive increase in its excess reserves. The Reserve Bank scaled up its liquidity operations through variable rate reverse repo auctions of a wide range of tenors from overnight to 91 days, absorbing liquidity (net) of 5.2 trillion. The Reserve Bank allowed oil bonds issued by the Government as eligible securities under the LAF. From the fortnight beginning November 26, an incremental CRR of 100 per cent was applied on the increase in net demand and time liabilities (NDTL) between September 16, 2016 and November 11, 2016 as a temporary measure to drain excess liquidity from the system. From November 28, liquidity absorption fell back and the Reserve Bank undertook variable rate repo auctions of 3.3 trillion on November 28. As expected, money market conditions tightened thereafter and the weighted average call rate (WACR) traded near the upper bound of the LAF corridor on that day before dropping back to the policy repo rate on November 30. All other rates in the system firmed up in sympathy, with term premia getting restored gradually.

Through this episode, active liquidity management prevented the WACR from falling even to the fixed rate reverse repo rate, the lower bound of the LAF corridor. Liquidity management was bolstered by an increase in the limit on securities under the market stabilization scheme (MSS) from 0.3 trillion to 6 trillion on November 29. There have been three issuances of cash management bills under MSS for 1.4 trillion by December 6, 2016."

Without further analysis or elaboration, let us take the message that when media and analysts were busy with the blame-game, India's central bank was doing its best to minimize the pains of demonetization not only to the common man by managing currency within the constraints but also to banking system and the economy in general.

Financial Sector Regulation

The Financial Sector Legislative Reforms Commission (FSLRC) went deep into several issues concerning financial sector regulators and GOI's debt management, but did not do much work on legislative reforms to improve the functioning of the institutional framework which is the conduit for resources mobilization and deployment of credit (banking business, in general). Thus, the institutional reforms, including licensing of new private sector banks, introduction of small banks and payment banks initiated during the Rajan Era in RBI, did not emanate from the recommendations of FSLRC.

The changes in the outreach, business pattern and expectations of the government of the day from different categories of financial institutions carrying out banking business during the current decade call for a re-look at the Banking Regulation Act to realign the regulatory requirements and methods of supervision to meet the current needs. Such a review will have to consider every aspect including capital adequacy, regulatory requirements, business priorities and specialization, outreach, HR issues and supervision of the institutional arrangement for banking in India.

HR Issues

The government should not further delay a revamp of the policy relating to recruitment, training, placement and compensation strategies across government, public and private sectors. A long-term solution may have to be found for HR-related problems, including inability to hire experts at market related compensation (this is applicable up to the position of secretary/CEO in government and public sector), skills becoming obsolete in short periods, employees' reluctance to change and demands from trade unions emanating from job security concerns. There may not be a "fit-for-all" remedy, as the issues are diverse and sometimes sector/institution-specific.

The government and public sector organizations may have to consider how best the "Cost to Company" (C to C) principles can be integrated into their existing recruitment, training, placement and career progression policies. This may involve convincing the existing employees that the changes will only improve the working results of the government departments and organizations they belong to and they will get opportunity to share the benefits and new job opportunities and so long as they are prepared to learn new things/upgrade their skills the infusion of 'experts' will not eat into their career progression opportunities. Inter-mobility of executives at higher levels among comparable departments of government and public and private sector organizations should be possible, on transparent norms and strictly based on merits.

Changes may have to come first in the recruitment and training procedures for IAS and relates services, management trainees in public/private sector undertakings including probationary officers in public sector banks (PSBs). Recent revamping of Tata Administrative Service gives enough food for thought for thinking on these lines. Specialized services like one for banking/financial sector could be evolved for institutions including those in the private sector and all regulatory bodies in the financial sector.

A transparent guidance for a remuneration package based on the paying capacity/need for skills for different sectors and ensuring social security should come from the government without always worrying about what will be the impact on cabinet secretary's salary or trade union demands. If the government secretary deserves a higher salary, the government should not raise budgetary concerns for not paying it. Instead, merger of some departments and utilizing the surplus manpower for new job opportunities should be a wiser option.

Time is opportune for both private and public sector organizations to have some introspection on their HR practices right from recruitment at the lowest level to the selection of CEOs, remuneration packages, training facilities and social security measures for their employees. While organizations in the private sector may have to review the optimum pressure they can put on their executives and managers, government and public sector counterparts may dispassionately examine and modify their remuneration packages to ensure attracting and retaining competitive talent in the present market scenario. Let us not forget that the civil services, executives and staff of public/private sector undertakings have to supplement the skills of the increasing number of political masters who were not as fortunate to get trained or groomed. The nation is immensely dependent on them for carrying out the development agenda on hand.

Till, perhaps ten years back, employers could depend on a growing population of educated unemployed from which they could hire and fire candidates on their terms. The position has changed with the opening up of the economy and sooner we realize it and act, the better. Dodging real issues could take us back to pre-reform days.

Silver Lining

There are positive indications coming from those responsible for advising GOI in matters relating to overhaul of HR policies in banks. According to media reports, on January 5, 2017, speaking on the occasion of business chamber Assocham's foundation day in New Delhi, Banks Board Bureau (BBB) chairman Vinod Rai observed that "Maybe we are not able to do much with the fixed part of the compensation package but on the variable part, we are hopeful that in the next financial year, we will be able to introduce a far more attractive package, with monetary or non-monetary benefits, to make it more attractive for professionals to enter into the PSB space."

Rai admitted that PSBs are facing a talent crunch, and entry of more universal and payment banks are expected to add to this, besides recognizing the need for longer tenure at top level in banks to infuse accountability in the system. Rai felt that executive directors or whole time directors or a CEO should be in position at an age where he has got a minimum of six years or more to go in the institution, so that he can be held accountable for decisions.

Rai can convince the policy makers to take good care of Public Sector Banks at this juncture both from balance sheet and human resources management angles, as they account for more than 70 per cent of the banking business in India and any sign of weakness in their functioning will have long term negative impact on the country's economic growth.

Cooperatives

Cooperatives across the country had more than their due share of problems post-demonetization. While primary (urban) cooperative banks whose functioning is similar to mini-commercial banks are regulated and supervised by RBI, the three/two tier structure of cooperatives comprising State and District Cooperative Banks and thousands of primary cooperative societies have multiple regulatory and supervisory oversight involving RBI, NABARD and Registrar of Cooperative Societies (State Government). There is urgency in finding a solution to a problem that has arisen due to continued neglect of an institutional system which has been serving the semi-urban and rural areas of the country, with all constraints. Re are no alternative conduits to ensure banking service to their clientele in semi-urban and rural areas. The cooperatives need to survive, and ssues like politicization, inadequate skills or problems arising from the dual control of cooperatives by Centre and states should be set aside by judiciary, governments and cooperatives themselves for a short period. There is need for cooperation among these agencies in solving the immediate problems the clientele of cooperatives are facing today.

Several short-cuts are being tried by state governments and cooperatives which can only lead to more complications. The short-cuts include bypassing DCCBs by state cooperative bank (as in Kerala), diverting the business now being done by cooperatives to other agencies and taking the problems to courts which helps in postponing decision-making. At this stage Centre should assert and empower state level task forces involving RBI, NABARD, banks and state governments to resolve the problems locally in a time bound manner.

Indian Banking System is Robust

Since the setting up of Reserve Bank of India in 1935 and introduction of the Banking Regulation Act, 1949 (which was partially made applicable to cooperatives in 1966 through legislation), the institutional system providing banking service in India has grown both in size and geographical coverage. GOI and RBI have ensured that depositors' money remained safe and remunerative in banks and credit flow is being regulated to ensure provision of adequate funds for development needs and economic growth. While there is always scope for improvement, vigilance of the regulator has ensured timely intervention whenever things went wrong in individual institutions or sectors preventing big bank failures. When smaller banks, many in the primary (urban) bank category faced problems mainly on account of mismanagement, damage was minimized by RBI by encouraging prompt liquidation/merger proceedings. While Indian banks are complying with international norms of capital adequacy and income recognition, a lesser known fact is the high reserve requirements (CRR and SLR) work as a support system for government borrowings and serve as a cushion in adverse situations. In sum, despite all criticism, Indian banking System is robust to meet the current challenges and the depositors' savings are safe, secure and remunerative, and will remain so, till such time the government becomes greedy and kills the golden goose by exercising falsely assumed ownership rights!

*****

SECTION III

Institutional Reforms

Banks' Mergers: Big is Beautiful!

"The importance of a strong and efficient financial system with an adequate geographical reach and diversified functional spread can hardly be underestimated in terms of our broader national objectives of growth, social justice and external viability. The financial system is perhaps the most important institutional and functional vehicle for economic transformation. Finance is indeed the bridge between the present and the future, and whether it be the mobilization of savings, or th ir effective, efficient and equitable allocation for investment, it is the success with which the financial system performs its function that sets the pace for the achievement of broader national objectives."

– M Narasimham,
Former Governor, RBI

It is interesting to observe that GOI and RBI are working together most harmoniously on several crucial issues affecting Indian Economy and more particularly on Financial Sector Reforms at a time when media and analysts are wasting precious resources to build stories on a rift between the Finance Ministry and RBI. Their joint initiatives that fructified during the recent months/years include setting up of Banks Board Bureau under Vinod Rai, constitution of Monetary Policy Committee with eminent professionals as members, concluding the merger of associate with SBI and a bold move to handle stressed assets of the banking system under mandated guidance from RBI. Finance Minister has strengthened the hands of RBI by giving out strong signals that actions taken and guidance provided by the central bank will get unreserved support from GOI. The stance taken by GOI that state governments considering dole outs in the form of loan waivers etc will have to also find resources for funding such measures has to be seen in this perspective. Of late, Finance Minister Arun Jaitley too has started being more liberal in expressing GOI's willingness to support RBI in performance of the central bank's responsibilities without let or hindrance.

The above background makes one say with confidence that "Together, GOI and RBI can" do wonders. The SBI-Associates Merger, which was dodged on several occasions in the past and executed quickly recently, is a success story which can become a case study. Hopefully, when the whole process gets complete, all the doomsayers including those who feared large scale job loss will be proved wrong. Let us remember, restructuring is not about 'closure of business,' but about realignment of structures to meet the needs of changing times and optimizing deployment of resources. Same applies to mergers also.

Unfortunately, financial sector reforms in India in the past suffered, all through, from the impact of a "blow hot, blow cold" approach not only from the policy makers and political leadership, but from mainstream media and analysts also. Diverse vested interests always tried to use any one of them or a combination from these agencies to dodge changes which they considered, may affect their profit motives. Reforms in any sector do not make sense independent of a pragmatic approach to institutional restructuring and infusion of professionalism in management.

Proposal for restructuring banks is not a novel idea, either. The Committee on the Financial System (Narasimham Committee I) which submitted its report on November 8, 1991 had this to say on the structure of the banking system:

"...The Committee is of the view that the system should evolve towards a broad pattern consisting of:
 a) 3 or 4 large banks (including the SBI) which could become international in character;
 b) 8 to 10 national banks with a network of branches throughout the country engaged in 'universal' banking;
 c) Local banks whose operations would be generally confined to a specific region; and
 d) Rural banks (including RRBs) whose operations would be confined to the rural areas and whose business would be predominantly engaged in financing of agriculture and allied activities.

The spirit of the recommendation above remains relevant even today and acceptance of its relevance by policy makers is evident in the tone of recent deliberations at the highest level. What is needed now is integrating the changes in the mix of institutions and the changes in approach that are necessary to take cognizance of the advances in technology.

RBI's Perception

The Reserve Bank of India Governor Urjit Patel while delivering the Kotak Family Distinguished Lecture at Columbia University in New York during the last week of April 2017 observed that the Indian banking system could be better off, if some public sector banks are consolidated to have fewer but healthier entities, as it would help in dealing with the problem of stressed assets, which he flagged as a challenge before the central bank today. He observed:

"As many have pointed out, it is not clear that we need so many public sector banks. The system could be better off if they are consolidated into fewer but healthier banks."

Dr. Patel was of the view that since there were cooperative banks and micro-financial institutions to provide community-level banking, some banks can be merged, as a quid pro quo for timely government technical injection.

Patel noted that a series of measures have been taken in the past year on resolving the problem of the non-performing assets (NPAs), including completion of a comprehensive asset quality review of the banks.

Patel said in the instance of the insolvency and bankruptcy code, the Reserve Bank of India (RBI) has been preparing actively for the next step in an orderly resolution and this will be undertaken concomitantly with the resolution of the weakest bank balance sheets under the aegis of a revised prompt corrective action framework. He felt that the public sector banks need to raise private capital from the market and reduce reliance on government largesse. Probably, sharing the burden of recapitalizing may make the institutions more responsible to the stakeholders. RBI Governor mentioned that this will be a good way to restore some market discipline and get the banks and their shareholders to more seriously care about management decisions.

Dwelling in some detail, Dr. Patel said that consolidation of banks could also entail sale of real estate where branches are redundant as well as offering voluntary retirement schemes to manage headcount and adding younger, digital—savvy personnel. Of course, these are all details which could be tied up, once GOI and RBI decides the direction. Dr. Patel strongly expressed the view that divestment in public sector banks would have a positive role for the sector and the measure would improve overall banking sector health.

Way Forward

The merger of associate banks with SBI has shown that all blames dumped on employees were misplaced. As a large geographical area remain still unbanked or under-banked, surpluses in terms of manpower released can easily be redeployed elsewhere. As public sector banks and private sector banks raise resources from the same source and by and large are expected to serve the same clientele, GOI should avoid the temptation to 'divide and rule' and encourage a level playing field for both categories of banks in terms of regulatory environment, functional autonomy, a self-regulated revenue-based remuneration package and professional management of human resources.

The need for reorganization of Indian banking infrastructure to rationalize functional responsibilities, presence and outreach is as old as nationalization of banks. All along, we had a touch and run or 'first-aid' approach to financial sector reforms. Committees and Commissions, periodically have made recommendations on this issue, but restricted mandates or selective approach in accepting recommendations have delayed a comprehensive look at structural alterations.

Even during the last four years when RBI was visibly serious about changes in the institutional system in the financial sector, measures were sporadic and didn't take a global view in the context of existing infrastructure and future needs. Thus we see new institutions coming up and making existing ones running for life, branches and ATMs of several banks crowding commercially developed zones while small towns, less posh urban and semi-urban areas as also rural India wait for reasonably acceptable banking services within reach.

The merger of associate banks with SBI has shown that all blames dumped on employees were misplaced. As a large geographical area remain still unbanked or under-banked, surpluses in terms of manpower released can easily be redeployed elsewhere. As public sector banks and private sector banks raise resources from the same source and by and large are expected to serve the same clientele, GOI should avoid the temptation to 'divide and rule' and encourage a level playing field for both categories of banks in terms of regulatory environment, functional autonomy, a self-regulated revenue-based remuneration package and professional management of human resources.

Writing on the subject Dr. Charan Singh had observed that long term and enduring solution to the present problems of PSBs would lie in a slew of measures, many of which were tried sporadically as quick-fix or first aid ones from time to time and suggested constitution of a High Powered Committee (HPC) to go into the whole issue of structural reforms in the banking sector. The HPC, if constituted should be a representative body of experts, stakeholders including GOI and RBI and employees' interests. While private sector participation should not be discouraged, at present stage of development, the public sector identity may have to be preserved to ensure the continued performance of priority and social sectors responsibilities by banking sector. The HPC could look into:

a) Merger of weak public/private sector banks with strong banks either in the public or private sector which are interested in expanding business.
b) Rationalizing branch network by initiating enabling legislative measures for closure/merger of branches in areas where there are more than necessary number of branches for historical reasons.
c) Rationalizing ATM network. Pooling of ATMs will save unnecessary maintenance expenditure including security costs.

d) HR issues including recruitment, career progression and remuneration packages in PSBs vis a vis their successful counterparts.
e) Focus on the need to ensure efficiency and autonomy in management at top level.
f) Possibility of lateral mobility of middle and top level executives across public sector and private sector banks and supervisory and regulatory bodies in the financial sector. Ideally, as early as possible, a Financial Sector Service comparable with other civil services should evolve.
g) Revisiting Lead Bank Scheme (LBS) to ensure that social responsibilities are not neglected. The LBS model of 1980's had certain ingredients like involvement of different stakeholders in resources mobilization and credit planning and ensuring a project approach in development activities.
h) Enforcing discipline in lending to big borrowers and transfer of business to other PSBs or private sector banks in geographical areas where a particular bank is not successful. Merger of loss-making or redundant bank branches with branches of other banks.
i) Possibility of lateral mobility of middle and top level executives across public sector and private sector banks and supervisory and regulatory bodies in the financial sector. Ideally, as early as possible, a Financial Sector Service comparable with other civil services should evolve.

Privatization not an Acceptable Option

The history and evolution of Indian banking sector during the last 4 decades do not take one to accept privatization of public sector banks as a solution for the present problems. With the exception of State Bank of India, Indian banking sector was under private ownership for decades after independence. The need to nationalise was felt in the context of the refusal of private sector to cater to the development needs of the country including taking banking service to semi-urban and rural areas and meeting the credit needsof small borrowers. Such responsibilities are still met by PSBs is evident from the fact that post-nationalisation, the residual and new private sector banks together could, till date, manage a market share of less than 30 per cent in the country's banking business.

*****

A Holistic Approach to PSBs' Merger

> *"You have to be careful in any kind of merger that you don't get a big weak bank! You'd hope that the strong bank would clean up the weak bank's problems but there are very few banks without problems today in the public sector. So, the question you have to ask is are there any dangers in distracting the bankers once again with a new set of issues such as headache with mergers and so on, and not resolving the real problem which is cleaning up their balance sheets."*
>
> – Raghuram Rajan,
> Former Governor, RBI

I had concluded my July 2017 article on bank mergers with the following observations:

"The history and evolution of Indian banking sector during the last 4 decades do not take one to accept privatization of public sector banks as a solution for the present problems. With the exception of State Bank of India, Indian banking sector was under private ownership for decades after independence. The need to nationalise major banks was felt in the context of the refusal of private sector to cater to the development needs of the country including taking banking service to semi-urban and rural areas and meeting the credit needs of small borrowers. Such responsibilities are still met by PSBs is evident from the fact that post-nationalisation, the residual and new private sector banks together could, till date, manage a market share of less than 30 per cent in the country's banking business."

At the risk of uncomfortable repetition, let me reiterate that there are certain sectors which will have to be nurtured for some more time by government, as leaving them entirely to the vagaries of the commercial interests of private sector will be perilous. These include healthcare, transport, education and banking. Therefore, we will take the debate forward on the premise that revamp of public sector banks (PSBs) will continue to be the responsibility of their present majority stakeholders, namely GOI.

Dr. Raghuram Rajan became RBI Governor at a time when India's central bank needed a leader who was willing to apply his own mind and did not always need guidance from North Block to lead Team RBI in the performance of mandated responsibilities. This helped RBI to take forward several initiatives which were on the drawing board since 1990's. Introduction of new institutions (payment banks, small banks, fresh commercial bank licenses), giving the status of "bank" to the banking business done by post offices, handling willful defaulters and stressed assets of banking system and sieving the Financial Sector Legislative Reforms Commission's report for rational and workable recommendations would not have happened this fast, but for Rajan's leadership. As his presence at Mint Road was destined to be short-term, restructuring and revamp of the existing banking structure didn't take off during his tenure. He, however, did have his own independent views on revamp of banking structure.

In an interview with the Hindu Business Line (published on September 7, 2017) Dr. Rajan responded to the specific question on 'the idea of merging the weak banks with stronger ones to contain the NPA mess' thus:

> "That may well be, but at this point your most urgent task is to clean up the banks and recapitalize them. Once they're on an even keel you can worry about that decision. But tell me, which are the mega projects that are waiting there to get financed by the big banks? It's not clear to me that our demand for investment is that strong right now. There might well be some obvious mergers, I haven't been looking at this in close detail. But I wouldn't use mergers as yet another way to escape the necessity for cleaning up and hope that somehow you put a stronger bank with a weaker bank and figure out a way to clean up. It's not clear to me that we have that many strong banks to believe that process will magically happen."

Inside RBI, time doesn't stand still. During the year Dr. Rajan was observing a self-imposed silence on India's central bank, Team RBI was coping with the legacy he had left with several open battle fronts and some bleeding wounds. RBI has an institutional identity and mind of its own and never took credit in shirking responsibilities and regretting in leisure. On demonetization, on mercilessly witnessing the depletion of RBI's reserves to an all time low during his tenure and procrastinating a long pending pension revision issue he inherited from his predecessors, Dr. Rajan followed the path of self-protection and expediency. In his recently released book "I Do What I Do" on page 211, he laments on his helplessness in resolving pension revision issue in RBI recording his regret openly:

"...On the internal front, my biggest regret is that I could not solve a long-pending matter that I inherited from my predecessors: securing for retired RBI staff the same pension benefits that government employees enjoy, despite repeated assurances from the government that the matter would be addressed. I hope the government will do the right thing here..."

But Reserve Bank of India takes things in its stride and moves forward.

RBI Deputy Governor Dr. Viral Acharya who was pleased to be identified as 'Poor man's Raghuram Rajan' before taking up the present job, concluded his 8th R K Talwar Memorial Lecture on "The Unfinished Agenda: Restoring Public Sector Bank Health in India" with the following observations:

"The Cabinet Committee on Economic Affairs has recently authorised an Alternative Mechanism to take decision on the divestment in respect of public sector banks through exchange-traded funds or other methods subject to the government retaining 52% stake. Synergistic mergers may also be part of the broader scheme of things. The Union Cabinet has also authorized an Alternative Mechanism for approving amalgamation of public sector banks. The framework envisages initiation of merger proposal by the Bank Boards based on commercial considerations, which will be considered for in-principle approval by the Alternative Mechanism. This could provide an opportunity to strengthen the balance sheets, management and boards of banks and enable capital raising by the amalgamated entity from the market at better valuations in case synergies eventually materialize. All of this is good in principle. There are several options on the table and they would have to work together to address various constraints. What worries me however is the glacial pace at which all this is happening. Having embarked on the NPA resolution process, indeed having catalyzed the likely haircuts on banks, can we delay the bank resolution process any further?"

After dwelling in some detail on the urgency to address the issue of restoring the financial health of PSBs, Dr. Acharya concluded that he was not comfortable with the slow pace at which the current initiatives are progressing and expressed the fear that time was running out. He mentioned that the *Indradhanush* was a good plan, but to end the Indian story differently, we need soon a much more powerful plan – "*Sudarshan Chakra*" – aimed at swiftly, within months if not weeks, for restoring public sector bank health, in current ownership structure or otherwise.

Consolidation and Restructuring an Ongoing Process

Banking Sector in India, during the pre-independence days, mainly catered to the needs of the government, rich individuals and traders. 1950's with a democratic government with a new outlook to planning and economic development saw GOI and RBI taking quick initiatives to exploit the potential of the banking system for mobilization of resources and channelizing their deployment in public interest opened its door wider and set out for the first time to bring the entire productive sector of the economy – large as well as small, in its fold. During this period number of commercial banks declined remarkably. There were 566 banks as on December, 1951; of this, number scheduled banks was 92 and the remaining 474 were non-scheduled banks. This number went down considerably to the level of 281 at the close of the year 1968. The sharp decline in the number of banks was due to heavy fall in the number of non-scheduled banks which touched an all time low level of 210. The banking scenario prevalent in the country up-to—the year 1968 depicted a strong stress on class banking based on security rather than on' purpose. Before 1968, only RBI and Associate Banks of SBI were mainly controlled by Government. Some associates were fully owned subsidiaries of SBI and in the rest, there was a very small shareholding by individuals and the rest by RBI.

The above recap is to emphasize that for RBI, equipping the Indian Financial System to meet the changing needs of India's economic development is always a 'work in progress' and given the policy support from the political leadership and GOI, the central bank has been remolding and reskilling the banking infrastructure and training the personnel responsible for implementing projects and programmes on an ongoing basis.

Raghuram Rajan has given a new direction to rebuilding the institutional structure supporting banking business in India during his short three year tenure as RBI Governor. Those who have been following RBI's history are aware that the introduction of new institutions and merger of existing one initiated by Rajan during 2013–16, were in fact a continuation of RBI's ongoing efforts to make Indian Banking System serve the financial sector better and more efficiently. Rajan didn't get the 'breathing time to convince India the rationale behind the introduction of new institutions (Payment Banks, Small Banks and conversion of Post Office Banking Buiness into a separate 'Postal bank') or to apply his mind to a holistic approach to the revamp of Public Sector Banks and Private Sector Banks which should have considered capital needs, structural reforms including mergers and amalgamations/closures of banks/branches and the roles of GOI and RBI in planning and implementing the 'best action plan.' In fact he started filling his backpack for his return journey to Chicago sometime during February/March, 2016.

Present Status

The finance ministry (read GOI) seems to be serious about taking up consolidation of public sector banks (PSBs) simultaneously with other measures aimed at improving the health of Indian Banking System. Each merger decision will be guided by various factors including financial performance of individual entities taken up for merger. These include regional balance, geographical reach, financial burden and smooth human resource transition. Care will also have to be taken to ensure that there should not be merger of a very big weak bank with a smaller strong one as it could adversely affect the financial health of the latter.

In the last consolidation drive, five associates and Bharatiya Mahila Bank (BMB) became part of SBI on 1 April 2017. The process helped State Bank of India to become one of the top 50 banks in the world. Besides BMB, State Bank of Bikaner and Jaipur (SBBJ), State Bank of Hyderabad (SBH), State Bank of Mysore (SBM), State Bank of Patiala (SBP) and State Bank of Travancore (SBT), were merged with SBI.

With the merger, the total customer base of the SBI reached around 37 crore with a branch network of around 24,000 and nearly 59,000 ATMs across the country. The merged entity began operations with deposit base of more than Rs. 26 lakh crore and advances level of Rs. 18.50 lakh crore.

Way Forward

Shankkar Aiyyar writing in The New Indian Express during July 2017 analysed the current merger proposal and inter alia made the following observations:

- Every season an old idea finds new life. The idea in currency currently is merger of public sector banks (PSBs). Branded as consolidation, the agenda is to reduce the number of government-owned banks by merging smaller banks into larger anchor banks—Bank of Baroda, Canara Bank, Punjab National Bank and Bank of India.

The road map for this consolidation, we are informed, is being worked out by the Niti Aayog.

- The promoted thesis is that there is no need for so many, that is, 21 PSBs. The bare-bone details of the proposal suggest that the objective is to bring down the number from 21 to 12.

Questioning the sanctity of 12 banks he posed the question: "Why not consolidate to five zonal banks, and do it now?"

Leaving Aiyyar and his arguments at this point, let us consider the rationale behind the current 'consolidation' efforts. Reading between the lines, there seems to be near convergence of thought processes among stakeholders on the following points in regard to merger of PSBs:

a) India doesn't need the present number of public sector banks with same pattern of ownership and management and using the same resources base and serving the same clientele from different 'offices.'

b) There is waste of infrastructure when same service is offered by multiple outlets with focus on the same clientele. While competition need to be encouraged, it should not be between institutions under the same ownership.

c) Stressed assets of the banking system need to be managed without affecting the credibility of the institutional system in the financial sector.

d) Weak banks/branches should have a smooth exit route. As there is enough potential to expand banking business to unbanked or

under-banked sectors and geographies, this may not pose insurmountable HR issues.
The challenge before GOI and RBI is how fast decisions are taken and implemented considering the above aspects and more.

*****

Small Banks, Big Expectations

The existing banking structure in India, comprising public sector banks including State bank of India and its Associate Banks, old and new private sector banks including the new entrant from the MFI family, namely Bandhan Bank, Regional Rural banks, Local Area Banks, primary (urban) cooperative banks, state and central cooperative banks dispensing credit through thousands of primary cooperative credit societies, evolved over several decades, is elaborate and has been serving the credit and banking services needs of the economy. This structure has multiple layers to cater to the specific and varied requirements of different customers and borrowers. The banking structure has been instrumental in the mobilisation of savings and promoting economic development in India. In the post financial sector reforms (1991) phase, the performance and strength of the banking structure has improved perceptibly.

Financial soundness of the Indian commercial banking system compares favourably with its counterparts in the advanced and emerging countries. The credit for this goes entirely to the post-independence political leadership of the country which allowed functional autonomy (RBI Governor

Dr. Raghuram Rajan recently referred to this as *'De facto* autonomy') to judiciary and the central bank all through, including during the stressed period of emergency, when democracy was in captivity. Reserve Bank of India on its part never assumed a confrontational position against GOI on any issue at any point of time. Instead, where felt necessary, RBI delayed implementation of its own decisions, which its professional wisdom approved as right, till it could take GOI into confidence. Such delays, at times have resulted in avoidable losses to the country and brought down the reputation of RBI by a shade. RBI top management has all along been taking the position of a caring teacher, when occasionally, some individuals in government assumed recalcitrant positions on crucial issues. The approach helped the central bank to play its regulatory and supervisory role with confidence.

This explains the philosophy behind RBI's moves in changes in regulatory norms and institution building in the financial sector. There is a general perception among analysts and economists who comment in the media about the recent moves by GOI and RBI to increase the banking network by introducing new players as something new. Let the records be put straight by mentioning that the process of reforms in the banking institutional structure is an ongoing one in India and within RBI, studies for making the performance of banks better are taken up from time to time.

The discussion paper "Banking Structure in India – The Way Forward" released by RBI during August 2013(accessible from RBI's website rbi.org.in) was the result of one such effort. The paper claimed that the primary motivation for the exercise of reviewing the Indian banking structure was to cater to the needs of a growing and globalizing economy as well as deepening financial inclusion, recognizing the importance of incorporating lessons from the global crisis, even when the Indian banking system had remained largely unaffected by the global crisis. The document gives the progress so far and RBI's thinking about the future of the country's banking structure.

Concept of Small Finance Banks

The proposal to licence small finance banks can be seen as a continuation of making certain provisions of Banking Regulation Act 1949 to cooperative societies through enactment of Banking Regulation Act (As Applicable to Cooperative Societies) during 1960's. Cooperative societies engaged in the business of banking and satisfying certain criteria were compulsorily brought under the purview of Banking Regulation Act and those which wanted to remain outside RBI regulation were given option to do so subject to certain conditions like 'not accepting deposits withdrawable by cheque.' After cooperative banks, Regional Rural banks (RRBs) and Local Area banks were set up in the small banks' category with specific mandates to cater to the savings and credit needs of certain categories of clientele which did not get adequate attention from bigger banks.

The new category of small finance banks now being licenced belong to a different category and there seems to be a new approach on the part of RBI in selecting the eligible applicants for issue of licence to this type of banks. The cautious stance while selecting new promoters for licensing big private sector banks and the effort to bring many players who are already doing banking-like business into mainstream banking seen in the selection of candidates for payment banks and small finance banks reveals a broad pattern in RBI's thinking. As the existing private sector banks (old and new generation) have not made much progress in increasing their share in banking business which remains at around 25 per cent, the balance being still with public sector banks, bringing more players may not help much in increasing outreach or promoting financial inclusion. Bringing existing players from the microfinance institutions (MFIs) and supporting organisations like India Post to instil professionalism in mobilisation of savings and providing credit to small borrowers make more sense.

Small Finance Banks and Financial Inclusion

More than three years back, I had concluded my first article in this magazine, which was on financial inclusion, with the following observation:

"The speed with which changes are brought about in the approach to governance and financial sector reforms will define the timeframe within which India will be able to come out of the present impasse. Coming out, India will. Present eruptive symptoms show that 'we, the people' will not show the patience with which they waited for generations to gain independence, for realizing basic human rights. Financial inclusion will expedite empowerment towards achieving this goal. The segment of the generation which benefited maximum from LPG

(Liberalisation-Privatisation-Globalisation) policies, those who were in the age group of 15–35, circa 1991 should take the responsibility to take India out of the mess in which the lazy generation to which I belong has landed the country. It will be in their self-interest."

I am looking back with satisfaction the developments on the economic front in recent times in our country.

Writing about this year's economics Nobel winner Angus Deaton, Justin Wolfers, professor at the University of Michigen makes the following observation about data:

"...For too long, econometric analysis had proceeded as if data were simply handed down from a statistician-loving higher power. The reality is far uglier: Data are imperfect, surveys can be unrepresentative, people misreport, and attempts to re-contact survey participants often fail. Deaton confronts these issues head-on, and he has taught economists how to extract meaning from imperfect data."

The quote is relevant not only in the context of the dilemma faced by planners, social scientists and regulators equally in understanding poverty and financial inclusion. Even the feedback given to Prime Minister Modi about the progress made in implementation of Pradhan Mantri Jan Dhan Yojana need to be viewed again, after going through this observation by Justin Wolfers. Prime Minister was informed that additional deposits of Rs. 32,000 crore had accrued into newly opened accounts under the scheme. PM said, *"Hum abhee tak ameeron ke gareebee dekhe hei... Ab hum gareebon ke ameeree dekha..."* (So far we have seen the poverty of the rich... Now we saw the wealth with the poor...) Without contesting facts, let us also remember that banks with lakhs of crores of deposit base, in any case will be opening new accounts and accepting fresh deposits. This is not to belittle the achievement under the scheme with provision for zero balance accounts for ensuring financial inclusion, but to view data with an open mind.

Way Forward

The RBI Discussion Paper of August 2013 is based on in-depth in-house studies and the present RBI position on future banking structure takes into account the findings of those studies. This enhances one's confidence in the central bank's professional competence in addressing various issues such as enhancing competition, financing higher growth, providing specialized services and furthering financial inclusion. It is in this context one has to view the present transition of the Indian banking system back to a new variety of multi-agency approach which has been covered in some detail, in the previous chapters.

*****

Back to Multi-Agency System

The current decade is going to see a churning of sorts in the Indian banking system, perhaps unparalleled in the history of the country's financial intermediation. Post-independence, simultaneously with the consolidation of hundreds of small territories governed by the British and local Maharajas, several financial institutions which called themselves banks also were merged and amalgamated to form new entities capable of meeting the emerging challenges, under the visionary leadership of RBI.

In 1991, the Committee on Financial Sector Reforms (Narasimham Committee) visualised a structure for Indian banking system with "three or four large banks that could become international in character, eight to ten banks with a network of branches throughout the country engaged in 'universal banking,' local banks whose operations would be generally confined to a specific region and rural banks (including Regional Rural Banks-RRBs) whose operations would be confined to the rural areas and whose business would be predominantly engaged in financing of agriculture and allied activities." It was not the Committee's mandate to make a comprehensive review of the revamp of the Indian financial sector institutional system which included, besides commercial banks, cooperatives – a three-tier system comprising state cooperative banks, district level central cooperative banks and primary agricultural credit societies-about a lakh of them, of various sizes and varying levels of financial health – and a multitude of entities which were engaged in mobilisation of financial resources and were engaged in promoting savings, engaged in investment and providing credit, many of which came to be known as Non-Banking Finance Companies and Microfinance Institutions. These were in addition to institutional financial intermediaries like post offices, insurance companies and government owned corporations in the business of resources mobilisation and investment in different ways. In India, there is no institution other than RBI which can have a 'holistic' approach to savings and credit.

Reserve Bank of India, with the active support of GOI, has been playing a significant role, without many parallels in the central banking history, in institution-building in the financial sector. Whatever be the assessment by the international rating agencies or spokespersons of private sector, during the three decades that followed independence, the support given to the public sector organisations in the core sector by GOI and the part played by RBI in reorganisation and effective supervision of banks in India have prepared the ground for the post-1990 reforms and the present optimism about India Growth Story which is being marketed with ease by us.

The period 1950 to 1990 saw in-depth studies like All India Rural Credit Survey, All India Rural Credit Review, Committee to Review the Arrangements for Institutional Credit for Agriculture and Rural development (CRAFICARD) and the study by the Agricultural Credit review Committee. Institutions like SBI, IDBI, NABARD and UTI at national level came into being with active participation and support from RBI and GOI during this period. The reorganization of cooperative credit system and setting up of 196 Regional Rural banks and massive branch expansion of commercial banks helped banking penetrate to semi-urban and rural areas in India. Recalled all these, to emphasize the importance of preserving and improving the existing outlets of financial intermediation while giving birth to new institutions in the financial sector. The country with 1.25 billion people, with majority of its population still fighting hunger and unemployment, can accommodate any number of new institutions, if they will cater to the real needs of the people. India can accommodate several Singapores and Hong Kongs and compete with not just China, but with US also, once the country decides to use its resources properly.

In the chapter "Governor' Overview" in RBI's Annual Report 2014–15, Dr. Raghuram Rajan made the following points:

"In the financial sector, we need to increase efficiency through greater entry and competition. The most appropriate institutions will prevail when the competitive arena is level, so we have to remove regulatory privileges as well as impediments wherever possible, especially those that are biased towards some form of ownership or some particular institutional form. We need more participation in our financial markets to increase their size, depth, and liquidity.

Participation is best enhanced not through subventions and subsidies but by creating supporting frameworks that improve transparency, contract enforcement, and protections for market participants against abusive practices."

Quoted here to draw attention to the RBI's vision about the institutional framework for banking in India that will evolve during the current decade. RBI's clarity of purpose is evident from the way in which the central bank is moving forward in defining the role of financial institutions in economic development. The signals can be seen in the following decisions, which I interpret here from a layman's point of view:

i. The caution with which RBI approached licensing of new private sector banks and the selection of two applicants for giving licences. The 'voluntary conversion' of Bandhan from a Microfinance Institution to a bank, hopefully, will pave the way for several so-called NBFCs to join the mainstream banking institutions by conversion, merger or amalgamation sooner than later. On August 23, 2015 Bandhan Bank started with 501 branches in 22 states, 50 ATMs, 1.43 crore accounts and a loan book of Rs. 10,000 crore brought forward from its MFI days.

ii. RBI was more liberal in giving licences to payment banks. But the selection of candidates in this case is indicative of the central bank's concern to bring all those who are actually in the business of banking (this include post offices) in different ways into the banking discipline. Discipline and law enforcement are not a bad words as is being made out by some quarters.

iii. This article is being written just before the announcement about small banks. I am optimistic about new entrants into this sector fulfilling their role expectations in the short and medium term and some of them growing to compete with their big brothers now worrying about 'poaching' and 'cannibalisation' when talking about new entrants to banking sector.

Challenges Before RBI

RBI's role in the economic growth of the country and in financial inclusion keeps growing. It has to preserve the strength of the existing institutional system comprising public sector banks, old and new private sector banks, RRBs, cooperative banks including over 1000 urban cooperative banks (some of which want to migrate to the commercial banking sector) and NBFCs while allowing entry and growth of a new set of entities. Any laxity in management of NPAs or inadequate credit flow to priority sector or the neglect of deposit insurance responsibilities (the one lakh limit per account for deposit insurance coverage was decided ages ago and in the present scenario of many private sector players and euthanasia being given to banks in the cooperative sector the raising of this limit should receive immediate attention) is seen as inefficient supervision by RBI.

Perhaps, the overburdening of RBI with expanding responsibilities is putting strain on the central bank which is struggling with finance ministry continuously breathing over its shoulders. The RBI Annual Report 2014–15 carries much evidence to prove this and I quote a couple of paragraphs on HR issues contained in the Governor's Overview (I invite readers to access the full report at rbi.org.in):

i. 46. RBI is an efficient organization, which has steadily reduced its employee count from 35,500 in 1981 to 16,700 today, even while performing ever increasing quantities of work. The surplus it generated from its activities this year is 659 billion, which has been paid out entirely to the Government. There is, of course, always scope for improvement. For example, to ensure that we meet our commitment to the public, we have put out on our website timelines within which the public can expect responses to applications made to RBI. We will monitor those timelines to ensure our staff delivers as promised.

ii. 47. A key factor in RBI's success has been a satisfied staff. In the past, RBI used to have no problem attracting junior officers, losing only an occasional officer who was successful in the IAS exam. Today, we lose more than we should be comfortable with. This is why a revamp of the professional challenges we offer our staff is very much needed, and we hope the changes outlined earlier will help us become a more attractive employer. In this regard, our review of compensation, as well as the long-pending improvement in pensions for our retirees also.

I would like to conclude this chapter drawing attention to a couple of paragraphs in the recent RBI report on Trend and Progress of Banking (Chapter on Banking and Other Financial Institutions) which I quote:

i. 14. RBI has also stepped away from micromanaging the functioning of the PSB Boards through regulations, allowing Boards to determine how they will carry out their responsibilities for strategic planning, risk management, accounting, *etc*. RBI has also liberalized the compensation of private bank Board members, while maintaining some checks, to ensure Board members are properly incentivized.

ii. 15. Because PSBs compete in the same market place for talent as do private sector banks and foreign banks, and because skill gaps are increasing middle management levels because of past hiring freezes, they will be unnecessarily hampered if they are unable to pay appropriate compensation to middle and senior managers, as well as Board members. Of course, higher pay should come with better accountability for performance. Given that many PSBs have higher overall costs than private sector banks performing similar activities, there is some scope for cost rationalization even while improving the pattern of compensation. At the same time, we should recognise that PSBs undertake public interest activities (like the rollout of accounts under the *Pradhan Mantri Jan Dhan Yojana*) that are not always fully compensated. Government should endeavour to keep the competitive playing field level by fully compensating banks for activities it wants undertaken in the public interest.

Epilogue

Interesting times are ahead for the banking sector in India. It has to change a lot in terms of skill, efficiency and penetration if it has to maintain at least the level of efficiency the sector displayed during the Lead Bank Scheme days when there was massive branch expansion to meet the rural and semi-urban credit needs. Today, the difference is, unlike the money lenders of those days, there is a network of efficient players in the financial market who are willing to enter the mainstream banking network, provided banks will accept them with honor.

*****

Bad Bank: Not a Good Idea?

Since independence GOI and RBI have revamped and rejuvenated existing institutions at various levels in the financial sector and established new ones wherever a need was felt. The makeover of Imperial Bank to State Bank of India at national level to recent emergence of Payment Banks at ground level and setting up of specialized institutions like IDBI, Exim Bank and NABARD are the result of the joint effort of GOI and RBI. Institutions so established have been playing their role fairly well. The present proposal to have a separate institutional arrangement for handling stressed assets of the banking system has built-in features which can be harmful for the financial sector in the long run. Put bluntly, besides acting as a disincentive for professionalizing appraisal and credit delivery and recovery departments of the banks, the institutionalization of 'stressed assets' can further weaken the supervisory and regulatory bodies in the financial system.

Economic Survey 2016–17 bases its argument supporting establishment of a Public Asset Rehabilitation Agency (PARA, now loosely referred to as 'Bad Bank' in common parlor) on the following grounds:

1. It's not just about banks, it's a lot about companies. So far, public discussion of the bad loan problem has focused on bank capital, as if the main obstacle to resolving TBS was finding the funds needed by the public sector banks. But securing funding is actually the easiest part, as the cost is small relative to the resources the government commands. Far more problematic is finding a way to resolve the bad debts in the first place.
2. It is an economic problem, not a morality play. Without doubt, there are cases where debt repayment problems have been caused by diversion of funds. But the vast bulk of the problem has been caused by unexpected changes in the economic environment: timetables, exchange rates, and growth rate assumptions going wrong.
3. The stressed debt is heavily concentrated in large companies. Concentration creates an opportunity, because TBS could be overcome by solving a relatively small number of cases. But it presents an even bigger challenge, because large cases are inherently difficult to resolve.
4. Many of these companies are unviable at current levels of debt requiring debt write-downs in many cases. Cash flows in the large stressed companies have been deteriorating over the past few years, to the point where debt reductions of more than 50 percent will often be needed to restore viability.

    The only alternative would be to convert debt to equity, take over the companies, and then sell them at a loss.
5. Banks are finding it difficult to resolve these cases, despite a proliferation of schemes to help them.

Among other issues, they face severe coordination problems, since large debtors have many creditors, with different interests.

If PSU banks grant large debt reductions, this could attract the attention of the investigative agencies. But taking over large companies will be politically difficult, as well.

6. Delay is costly. Since banks can't resolve the big cases, they have simply refinanced the debtors, effectively "kicking the problems down the road."

    But this is costly for the government, because it means the bad debts keep rising, increasing the ultimate recapitalization bill for the government and the associated political difficulties. Delay is also costly for the economy, because impaired banks are scaling back their credit, while stressed companies are cutting their investments.

7. Progress may require a PARA. Private Asset Reconstruction Companies (ARCs) haven't proved any more successful than banks in resolving bad debts. But international experience shows that a professionally run central agency with government backing – while not without its own difficulties – can overcome the difficulties that have impeded progress.

The observations "Like all financial firms, central banks hold capital to provide a buffer against the risks they take... Measuring these risks and calculating how much buffer should be provided against them is difficult. For that reason, central bank capital holdings vary widely. RBI is an outlier (in shareholder equity to assets ratio) with an equity share of about 32 per cent, second only to Norway and well above that of the US Federal Reserve Bank and the Bank of England, whose ratios are less than 2 per cent. If the RBI were to move even to the median of the sample (16 per cent), this would free up a substantial amount of capital to be deployed for recapitalizing the PSBs," contained in the Economic Survey 2015–16 was contested on grounds of accuracy of facts and the then RBI Governor Dr. Raghuram Rajan had offered to guide those who wrote Economic Survey to understand RBI Balance Sheet (Dr. Rajan kept his word and did exactly what he promised, in a speech he delivered in Delhi the day before he completed his three year tenure as RBI Governor and returned to academia. See **Appendix 1**).

Suffice to say, those who are aware of the interlink between RBI's balance sheet and GOI finances are not in favour of using the RBI's capital and reserves to fund the non-performing assets (NPAs) of public sector banks.

Budget 2017–18

Finance Minister Arun Jaitley in his Budget speech made the following observations:

"The focus on resolution of stressed legacy accounts of Banks continues. The legal framework has been strengthened to facilitate resolution, through the enactment of the Insolvency and Bankruptcy Code and the amendments to the SARFAESI and Debt Recovery Tribunal Acts. In line with the *'Indradhanush'* roadmap, I have provided 10,000 crores for recapitalisation of Banks in 2017–18. Additional allocation will be provided, as may be required.

Listing and trading of Security Receipts issued by a securitization company or a reconstruction company under the SARFAESI Act will be permitted in SEBI registered stock exchanges. This will enhance capital flows into the securitization industry and will particularly be helpful to deal with bank NPAs."

FM doesn't look keen on taking forward the Economic Survey ideas about managing stressed assets so soon. In a post-budget interview, he said a bad bank is a potential solution but it cannot be supported by the government alone. He also said that he won't be able to comment on what solution will eventually emerge. Possibly Jaitley has in view the impact of bad bank funding on macroeconomic stability. The finance minister has committed to a fiscally balanced budget with a fiscal deficit target of 3.2% for 2017–18, government-debt-to-gross domestic product (GDP) target of 60% by 2023 and net market borrowing target of Rs. 3.5 trillion in 2017–18. These commitments do not account for bad bank funding.

The creation of a bad bank will put pressure on government finances at least initially. Even if the government funds only 20% of stressed assets in the banking system, it would have a heavy impact on the net market borrowing target in 2017–18. This will adversely affect achieving committed targets for fiscal deficit and government-debt-to-GDP ratio.

On March 15, 2017, addressing the first meeting of the Consultative Committee constituted by the Reserve Bank of India, attached to the Ministry of Finance, FM Jaitley said that dealing with NPAs was a challenging task. According to him the he core problem of NPAs was with very large corporates, though few in numbers, predominantly in the steel, power, infrastructure and textile sectors. On the issue of setting up a 'bad bank,' Jaitley said that several possible alternatives exist and the issue is being debated on public platforms. The government was also considering setting up more Oversight Committees that would look into cases referred to it by different banks.

Reserve Bank's Perception

Speech delivered by RBI Deputy Governor Viral Acharya at the Indian Banks' Association Banking Technology Conference held in Mumbai, on February 21, 2017 would guide us on the present thinking within RBI about handling stressed assets of banking system. Viral Acharya said there is a "sense of urgency" to decisively resolve Indian banks' stressed assets. One of his proposed solutions is the creation of a Private Asset Management Company (PAMC) for sectors in which assets are economically unviable in the short-to-medium term, like the power sector. Acharya feels, this plan would be suitable for sectors where the stress is such that assets are likely to have economic value in the short run, with moderate levels of debt forgiveness.

Let us not Institutionalize a Bad Idea

The bad bank idea, which was mooted last year didn't find favour with the then RBI governor Raghuram Rajan. The change of guard at Mint Road together with the compulsions arising from the severity of the bad loan problem plaguing the system, which has not so far been responding much to normal 'treatment,' helped media and analysts to make a second attempt.

Theoretically, a bad bank or an asset management company could be set up with government money to buy non-performing assets from banks. By transferring dead loans to the bad bank, banks become free of providing for these loans and making efforts to recover whatever is left recoverable. This would also free up precious capital which could then be used to boost credit flow to industry. But, banks with huge amount of stressed assets are also big enough to do whatever a newly constituted institution can do to make them perform or close the accounts after recovery of whatever part is recoverable. With appropriate legislative and legal support from GOI in the same manner banks form consortiums to lend to large projects banks can make joint efforts to pool resources and make joint recovery efforts. Such joint efforts will reduce the chances of borrowers shifting from one bank to another for softer treatment in regard to financial discipline.

Any proposal to institutionalize stressed assets raise questions like, who will pay for the potential losses? If banks are willing to sell loans at a haircut, wouldn't it make more sense to allow asset reconstruction firms, which have the required expertise in this area, to be major players?

Like the disinclination to repay unleashed by agricultural loan waivers, the very concept of a GOI-owned "bad bank" does create the problem of moral hazard as it creates incentives for banks to be reckless. The responsibility to recover or 'provide for' loans disbursed going bad should remain with the lender. Shifting this responsibility to another institution and funding the losses from taxpayers' money raises the more serious question of public perception and potential damage to the government's reputation.

*****

Appendix 1
(See Section III Chapter 5)

First Year Economics: There is no Free Lunch: RBI Dividend Policy[*]

A fundamental lesson in economics is there is no free lunch. This can be seen in the matter of the RBI dividend: Some commentators seem to suggest that public sector banks could be recapitalized entirely if only the RBI paid a larger dividend to the Government. Let me explain why matters are not so simple.

If what follows is complicated, trust me, it is. But pay attention, students, especially because it is about your money. I am sure you will understand. How does the RBI generate surplus profits?

We, of course, print the currency held by the public, as well as issue deposits (i.e. reserves) to commercial banks. Those are our fixed liabilities. As we issue these liabilities, we buy financial assets from the market. We do not pay interest on our liabilities. However the financial assets we hold, typically domestic and foreign government bonds, do pay interest. So we generate a large net interest income simply because we pay nothing on virtually all our liabilities.

---

[*] *Excerpts from remarks by Raghuram G Rajan, Governor, Reserve Bank of India on September 3, 2016 at St Stephen's College, New Delhi.*

Our total costs, largely for currency printing and banker commissions,

Amount to only about 1/7th of our total net interest income. So we earn a large surplus profit because of the RBI's role as the manager of the country's currency. This belongs entirely to the country's citizens.

Therefore, after setting aside what is needed to be retained as equity capital to maintain the creditworthiness of the RBI, the RBI Board pays out the remaining surplus to the RBI's owner, the Government.

The RBI Board has decided it wants the RBI to have an international AAA rating so that RBI can undertake international transactions easily, even when the Government is in perceived difficulty – in the midst of the Taper Tantrum, no bank questioned our ability to deliver on the FCNR (B) swaps, even though the liability could have been tens of thousands of crores. Based on sophisticated risk analysis by the RBI's staff, the Board has decided in the last three years that the RBI's equity position, currently around 10 lakh crores, is enough for the purpose. It therefore has paid out the entire surplus generated to the Government, amounting to about Rs. 66,000 crores each in the last two years, without holding anything back. This is of the order of magnitude of the dividends paid by the entire public sector to the Government.

In my three years at the RBI, we have paid almost as much dividend to the government as in the entire previous decade. Yet some suggest we should pay more, a special dividend over and above the surplus we generate. Even if it were legally possible to pay unrealized surplus (it is not), and even if the Board were convinced a higher dividend would not compromise the creditworthiness of the RBI, there is a more fundamental economic reason why a special dividend would not help the Government with its budgetary constraints.

Here's why: Much of the surplus we make comes from the interest we get on government assets or from the capital gains we make off other market participants. When we pay this to the government as dividends, We are putting back into the system the money we made from it – there is no additional money printing or reserve creation involved. But** when we pay a special dividend to the government, we have to create additional permanent reserves, or more colloquially, print money.

Every year, we have in mind a growth rate of permanent reserves consistent with the economy's cash needs and our inflation goals. Given that budgeted growth rate, to accommodate the special dividend we will have to withdraw an equivalent amount of money from the public by selling government bonds in our portfolio (or alternatively, doing fewer open market purchases than we budgeted). Of course, the Government can use the special dividend to spend, reducing its public borrowing by that amount. But the RBI will have to sell bonds of exactly that amount to the public in order to stick to its target for money creation.

The overall net sale of Government bonds by the Government and the RBI combined to the public (that

---

** *This is not strictly true. Our earnings on foreign exchange assets come from outside the system, so when we pay this to the Government as dividend, we are printing additional money. We do account for this.*

is, the effective public sector borrowing requirement) will not change. But the entire objective of financing Government spending with a special RBI dividend is to reduce overall Government bond sales to the public. That objective is not achieved!

The bottom line is that the RBI should transfer to the government the entire surplus, retaining just enough buffers that are consistent with good central bank risk management practice. Indeed, this year the Board paid out an extra 8,000 crores than was promised to the Government around budget time.

Separately, the government can infuse capital into the banks. The two decisions need not be linked. There are no creative ways of extracting more money from the RBI– there is no free lunch! Instead, the Government should acknowledge its substantial equity position in the RBI and subtract it from its outstanding debt when it announces its net debt position. That would satisfy all concerned without monetary damage.

If what I have said just now seems complicated, it is, but it is also the correct economic reasoning. Similar detailed rationales lead us to turn down demands to cut interest rates in the face of high inflation, to depreciate or appreciate the exchange rate depending on the whim of the moment, to use foreign exchange reserves to fund projects, to display forbearance in classifying bad loans or waived farmer loans as NPAs, and so on...

We have been tasked with a job of maintaining macroeconomic stability, and often that task requires us to refuse seemingly obvious and attractive proposals. The reason why we have to do what we have to do may not be easy for every unspecialized person, even ones with substantial economics training, to grasp quickly.

Of course, we still must explain to the best of our ability but we also need to create a structure where the public trusts the central bank to do the right thing. This then is why we need a trusted independent central Bank.

*****

PSBs' Recapitalization Gets on Track

Union finance minister Arun Jaitley by announcing the comprehensive recapitalization plan for public sector banks has done a commendable service to the banking system. The sagging image of Indian Banking System which had shouldered the major burden of the cleansing process of Indian Economy initiated by RBI and GOI last year has got a deserving boost by this timely measure. The Finance Minister gave the following details about the recapitalization plan for state-run banks worth Rs. 2.11 lakh crore approved by the Union Cabinet:

- Of Rs. 2.11 lakh crore, a sum of Rs. 1.35 lakh crore will be raised through recapitalization bonds while another Rs. 76,000 crore would be available from budgetary support and raised through market borrowings.
- The exact nature of these recapitalization bonds will be released later and the capital infusion plan may run into the next fiscal year.

Jaitley, during the press briefing about the recapitalization plan attributed the recent visible rise in NPAs to their being swept under the carpet till 2015, from when transparency came and indiscriminate lending by state-run banks between 2008 and 2013.

He added that the banks now have adequate lending capacity post demonetization.

Mainstream media has never been kind to Public Sector in general and Public Sector Banks in particular. A business magazine concluded its editorial last month (November 6–9, 2017 issue) with these words:

"We at......have long been skeptical of any real change, without real privatization. People (and even the BJP) forget that the BJP opposed Mrs. Gandhi's nationalization of the banks. And one only has to compare the value creation in the last two decades by private sector banks, compared with the huge value destruction in the public sector. We have also repeatedly pointed out that banking is an industry which is over 200 years old in India, and where we have a natural advantage.

It is this opportunity that a newly energized finance minister must sieze."

Good enough cocktail of facts, fiction and history to confuse a NewGen reader. Before moving forward, we will have a look at the major claim about 'value addition.' This value addition has happened only for the capital invested by 'private' owners of the private sector banks. Even the institutions have not benefited. Look at the growth in the business share or benefits passed on to borrowers in terms of interest rates reduction by bringing down net interest margins (NIM) by big private sector banks.

The argument against poor management of Public Sector Banks (PSBs) by their owner, namely GOI is not without basis. PSBs with the exception of SBI and its Associates (now merged into SBI) came into being through nationalization of private sector banks. Post-Nationalization, as the prime objective of nationalization was to make banks deploy the resources mobilized from public for the benefit of the public, in effect, management of PSBs were handed over to bureaucrats who were accountable only to the political leadership which controlled government. Professionalism was conspicuous by its absence from bank board rooms down to appraisal of loan proposals. Political parties in power both in Delhi and in states started using banks for implementing populist projects and forced waiver of loans when they became bad. The need of the hour is de-politicisation of banking business and infusing professionalism in the working of banks. The solution lies in providing a level playing field for PSBs and their private sector counterparts in management and business decisions within the contours of national policy in regard to prioritization of credit flow and ensuring geographical spread of bank branches. There is no escape from banking sector reforms.

Unlike other institutions, even the public sector – private sector divide does not make much sense in the case of banking business. Leaving the relatively small capital, for major portion of the resources both categories of banks depend on deposits from public/government. Considering the nature of service they provide as part of business, namely lending to earn returns and managing funds mobilized keeping the depositors' interest in view, banks in private and public sectors have to work with equal professionalism.

RBI Welcomes Recapitalization

Reserve Bank of India Governor Urjit Patel has welcomed the bank recapitalization plan announced by GOI. In the statement issued soon after announcement of Recapitalization Plan by the Finance Minister, Governor said in a statement (See **Appendix 2**) that "A well-capitalized banking, and in general, financial intermediation, system is a pre-requisite for stable economic growth. Economic history has shown us repeatedly that it is only healthy banks that lend to healthy firms and borrowers, creating a virtuous cycle of investment and job creation." Adding that, "For the first time in last decade, we now have a real chance that all the policy pieces of the jigsaw puzzle will be in place for a comprehensive and coherent, rather than piece-meal, strategy to address the banking sector challenges."

CAG's Perception

A recent Performance Audit Report covering the working of Public Sector Banks released by the Comptroller and Auditor General, inter alia, made the following observations:

- Public Sector Banks (PSBs) account for over 70 per cent of the deposits received in and advances made by Scheduled Commercial Bank (SCBs). The capital requirement of PSBs is driven by credit growth in the economy and prudential regulatory requirements. The regulatory framework for banks is globally framed by the Basel Committee on Banking Supervision which is adopted by RBI for Indian banks. Over 2008–16, the advances of PSBs have more than doubled, from Rs. 22,59,212 crore to

Rs. 55,93,577 crore, though the rate of increase in advances had decreased from 19.56 per cent in 2009–10 to 2.14 per cent in 2015–16.

- The return on assets (ROA) of PSBs which is a measure of their profitability has been consistently lower than that of SCBs (2011–16). PSBs account for nearly 88 per cent of Gross Non-Performing Assets (GNPAs) of the banking sector in 2015–16. There is a significant gap between book value and market value of PSB shares, with most PSBs having a lower market value which may come in the way of PSBs approaching the market for additional capital funds. II Infusion of Capital Funds by GOI in PSBs GOI infused Rs. 1,18,724 crore in PSBs during 2008–09 to 2016–17.
- The basis for working out parameters for capital infusion changed between actual and estimated values from year to year and often within different tranches in the same year (2010–11, 2015–16 and 2016–17). For FY 2014–15, there was a shift from 'need based' to 'performance based' capital infusion, with ROA being employed as the basic criteria for capital infusion.
- As per Indradhanush plan, for FY 2015–16, 20 per cent of the earmarked capital infusion was to be allocated to PSBs based on their performance during three quarters in FY 2015–16, which was not adhered to on account of the Asset Quality Review by RBI.
- In FY 2011–12, SBI was the only PSB which was infused with Rs. 7,900 crore, over and

above the regulatory requirement being 5,874 crore, on grounds that with impending norms of Basel III, SBI would be required to maintain a 11 per cent Tier I CRAR target. The 11 per cent norm for SBI was not followed in future years. During 2013–14, four PSBs which had a GOI shareholding above 58 per cent and did not require capital to meet the Tier I CRAR target, were infused with capital to the tune of Rs. 2,900 crore. This was done even as the requirement of 11 PSBs to meet the Tier I CRAR target, was not fully met. Against a target under Indradhanush for raising capital from the market by PSBs to the tune of Rs. 1,10,000 crore between 2015–16 and 2018–19, during January 2015 – March 2017, only Rs. 7,726 crore could be raised.

Bleeding Wounds

Though no one would like to question the noble intentions behind several initiatives taken by Dr. Raghuram G Rajan during his relatively short stay in India as RBI Governor, fact remains that several corrective and transplantation surgeries he initiated have left the Indian Financial Sector bleeding with several open wounds. As he would later claim, he did what he did, with conviction. Rajan had done his homework much before he took charge as RBI Governor and he could start working in full swing right away on September 4, 2013 and he maintained the tempo right up to the first week of September 2016 when he left for Chicago. He had a pragmatic approach to revamping the institutional structure in the financial sector, giving new content and meaning to Monetary Policy and most importantly handling the NPA menace which had gripped Indian banks. There are no comforting indications from Mint Road now to feel convinced that all the good initiatives taken during the 'Rajan Era' are being pursued with vigour towards their original objectives.

Made these observations in the context that the proposed Bank-Recapitalization is like a transplantation surgery. The difference here is the organ (funds for recapitalization) for transplantation is being removed from the same body (Indian Economy) into which it is being transplanted. In such a situation maintaining the health of Indian Economy and the Banking System which forms part of it becomes more significant. Simply put, structural reforms of banks, infusion of professionalism into the working of banks or banking reforms in general have gained urgency at this stage.

*****

Appendix 2
(See Section III Chapter 6)

Statement Issued by RBI Welcoming Bank Recapitalization Plan

RBI welcomes bank recapitalization plan. A well-capitalized banking, and in general, financial intermediation, system is a pre-requisite for stable economic growth. Economic history has shown us repeatedly that it is only healthy banks that lend to healthy firms and borrowers, creating a virtuous cycle of investment and job creation. The Government of India's decisive package to restore the health of the Indian banking system is in the view of the Reserve Bank of India (RBI), a monumental step forward in safeguarding the country's economic future. For the first time in last decade, we now have a real chance that all the policy pieces of the jigsaw puzzle will be in place for a comprehensive and coherent, rather than piece-meal, strategy to address the banking sector challenges. It bodes us well that this step has been taken in a time of sound macroeconomic conditions for the economy on other fronts. The proposed recapitalization package for the banking sector combines several desirable features. First, by deploying recapitalization bonds, it will front-load capital injections while staggering the attendant fiscal implications over a period of time. As such, the recapitalization bonds will be liquidity neutral for the government except for the interest expense that will contribute to the annual fiscal deficit numbers. Second, it will involve participation of private shareholders of public sector banks by requiring that parts of the capital needs be met by market funding. Last but not the least, it will allow for a calibrated approach whereby banks that have better addressed their balance-sheet issues and are in a position to use fresh capital injection for immediate credit creation can be given priority while others shape up to be in a similar position. This provides for a good way of bringing some market discipline into a public recapitalization program compared to the past recapitalization programs. Financial sector policies should support growth while maintaining financial stability. On behalf of the Reserve Bank of India, I commend the government on its bold steps in this direction, starting with implementation of the Insolvency and Bankruptcy Code that is helping resolve the underlying corporate stress, and culminating in yesterday's announcement of the public sector bank recapitalization program. The RBI looks forward to working with the Government to ensuring these plans reach their natural completion to the benefit of the broader Indian economy.

– Urjit R. Patel
Governor

SECTION IV

Stressed Assets in Indian Economy

Management of Stressed Bank Assets

"All countries have central banks, and some countries also have additional financial supervisory authorities with designated functions. These agencies are responsible for ensuring compliance with their rules and regulations, and thereby encouraging ethical behavior in dealings between banks and their borrowers and depositors. While rules and regulations as well as periodic inspections are necessary parts of the regulatory framework, the supervisory system in many countries has become overloaded, and is also highly bureaucratic an discretionary..."

– Bimal Jalan,
Former Governor, RBI

"The financial sector is, in many ways, the brain of a modern economy. When it functions well, it allocates resources and risk efficiently and thereby boosts economic growth while also making lives easier, safer and more fulfilling. It broadens opportunity and attacks privilege. It works for all of us. Of course, when it works poorly, as it has done recently,

it can do enormous damage while benefitting a very few."

– Dr. Raghuram Rajan in his book 'Fault Lines' (2010)

Recalled the above observations in the context of the challenges before Reserve Bank of India in the context of a surgical procedure which the central bank has been 'mandated' to oversee, to restore the health of the Indian Financial System.

Putting the 'Act' Together

On May 4, 2017, President of India gave his consent to an Ordinance amending the Banking Regulation Act, 1949 enabling Reserve Bank of India to initiate certain fresh measures for resolution of stressed assets in the banking system. The Banking Regulation (Amendment) Ordinance, 2017 inserted the following two sub-sections, after section 35A in the Banking Regulation Act, 1949:

35AA. The Central Government may by order authorize the Reserve Bank to issue directins to any banking company or banking companies to initiate insolvency resolution process in respect of a default, under the provisions of the insolvency and Bankruptcy Code, 2016.

Explanation – For the purposes of this section, "default" has the same meaning assigned to it in clause (12) of section 3 of the insolvency and Bankruptcy Code, 2016.

1. 35AB. Without prejudice to the provisions of section 35A, the Reserve Bank may, from time to

time, issue directions to the banking companies for resolution of stressed assets.
2. The Reserve Bank may specify one or more authorities or committees with such members as the Reserve bank may appoint or approve for appointment to advise banking companies on resolution of stressed assets.'

Role of RBI

Since independence, RBI has been performing several roles which are not assigned to Central Banks elsewhere in the world. The present Ordinance doesn't add much to the regulatory powers or responsibilities, but will serve to tell the stakeholders that GOI and RBI are on the same page, at least on the management of stressed assets by banks. RBI Act together with the pre-ordinance B R Act confer enough powers on RBI to regulate and supervise Banking System. Problems, including the present one relating to stressed assets emanated from back-seat driving by Finance Ministry using "ownership rights" both that of RBI and PSBs. Trespass into internal functioning including credit decisions and HR issues by finance ministry during the 10 years ending FY 2014 has done irreparable damage to the functioning of RBI and PSBs. Unusual situations call for unusual policy decisions. Ordinance should be seen in this perspective.

According to some interpreters, the NPA ball has been kicked back to RBI's court. Let us take on record that the above Ordinance doesn't differentiate between public sector banks and private sector banks. And, it would be foolish to comment on the brief amendments to B R Act carried out through the Ordinance, in isolation.

Experts' View

These days, sane pieces of advice on policy, which are not guided by constituency interests, are a rarity. But, an interview with Deepak Parekh, Chairman, HDFC captioned 'RBI has to ensure NPAs are not swept under the carpet' published in a mainstream financial daily (Business Standard) on May 16, 2017 proves that there is still scope for hope and there will be appreciation from those who understand things, if policy makers and regulators move in the right direction.

The brief answers from the veteran banker, to the pertinent questions raised by Joydeep Ghosh should set at rest the apprehensions raised by economists and the analysts in the media about the purport of the Ordinance amending the B R Act and the role of RBI in the resolution of NPA crisis.

Post-Ordinance debates strayed away from the main issue of managing stressed assets of the banking system and were sometimes judgmental about the modalities to be followed and the role of GOI and RBI in supporting the banks to get out of a crisis created by policies which compromised prudent principles of banking for political and administrative expediency.

Deepak Pareekh has done a service to the future of the Indian Financial System by making the following observations:

a) 'It is a pointless debate over whether banks are giving up their autonomy or whether the RBI or the government will be micro-managing the situation...it is the job of the regulator to ensure stability in the system.'

b) 'With the benefit of hindsight, it (RBI being aggressive on the asset quality review) was the right decision as the AQR brought out the extent of toxic assets in the system. Where the central bank needs to firmly stand its ground is putting an end to the practice of sweeping NPAs under carpet. This, above all, is an issue of governance.'

All Blame on PSBs

Public sector banks continue to remain the whipping boy for the non-performance of assets created in the private sector. The context in which they came into existence in the first place, and the reluctance of residual and new private sector banks to finance social or priority sectors or even look at clientele below a certain threshold levels they arbitrarily fix or open shops in semi-urban and rural areas.

All through, the comparisons have been the percentages of gross and net NPAs accumulated in 'public' and 'private' sector banks and 'market valuation' of the two categories of banks. Rarely one reads anything about the context of formation of State Bank of India, Bank Nationalization, current business mix or share in banking business held by the two categories of banks. Remember, both categories of banks are sourcing their resources from public deposits and are expected to serve the same clientele.

RBI Initiative

Stricter and prudent classification of stressed assets at the instance of RBI doesn't change the health of such assets. If PSBs are to continue to perform the role expectations of nationalization, they need a level playing field in choice of clientele, area of operation, sectors to be financed and more importantly in managing HR related issues including recruitment and compensation packages of staff. If some un-remunerative or loss-making sectors including agriculture or social sectors have to be financed by banks for policy reasons, they should be identified by GOI and entrusted to banks for financing on mutually agreed terms, which will include compensation for losses. Here the criterion should be specialization in work and not a differentiation between public and private sector banks.

Major portion of the so called "stressed assets of banks" are in the private sector, and all of us continue to blame the banking regulator and the Public Sector Banks which are abused as conduits for mobilization of deposits from the public and transferring the public resources to private hands by design. If citizens decided to keep their hard earned savings only with the trustworthy, reliable private sector banks (In sum this is the impression analysts are trying to build up in the minds of depositors!) only, how public sector banks will misuse public funds? Taking this debate forward will be in public interest.

Reserve Bank of India has initiated informed debate on these issues during 2013–16 when Dr. Raghuram Rajan was Governor and we are fortunate to have institutional continuity in policy perceptions at Mint Road through Dr. Rajan's successor Dr. Urjit Patel and the toung Deputy Governor Dr. Viral Acharya who succeeded Dr. Patel. Viral Acharya in a recent (April 28, 2017) speech made the following observations:

"We keep hearing clarion calls for more and more government funding for recapitalization of our public sector banks. Clearly, more recapitalization with government funds is essential. However, as a majority shareholder of public sector banks, the government runs the risk of ending up paying for it all. The expectation of government dole outs might have been set by the past practice of throwing more money after the bad. Take for instance our bank recapitalization plan of 2008–09 after the global financial crisis: banks that experienced the worst outcomes received the most capital in a relative sense. Most of these banks need capital again."

It was in this background that Dr. Acharya in his maiden speech after taking over as RBI Deputy Governor mentioned about various options to handle stressed assets. In his speech delivered at the Indian Banks' Association Banking Technology Conference, on February 21, 2017, Dr. Acharya observed:

"Let me mention the key principles to successful restructuring that I have managed to glean:

First, there has to be an incentive provided to banks to get on with it and restructure the stressed assets at a price that clears the market for these assets. If they don't do it in a timely manner, then the alternative should be costlier in terms of the price they receive.

Second, the ultimate focus of restructuring and of assessment as to whether the restructuring package being offered tothe bank is at the "right" price must be the efficiency and viability of the restructured asset. Generating the best price for the bank at all costs may only result in cosmetic changes and risk serial non-performance of the assets.

Third, not all of the resulting bank losses should simply be footed by the government. As a majority shareholder of public sector banks, the government runs the risk of ending up paying for it all.

It should manage the process at the outset to avoid that outcome.

Wherever possible, private shareholders of banks should also be asked to chip in. Some surgical restructuring should be undertaken to consolidate and strengthen bank balance-sheets so that private capital will come in at better valuations. It might have to accept that it is best to let some banks shrink over time. Divestments should also be on the table.

Historically, significant restructuring of stressed assets has almost always involved significant bank restructuring."

Stakeholders

Till recently, the three biggest stakeholders of banks, namely, the bank employees, the savers (depositors) and bank borrowers have remained mere spectators when various policy decisions were thrust on banks by government which, in one way or the other affected their interests. During the last two years, some awakening, which is a positive signal is visible.

Bank employees are daring to tell publicly that government cannot enforce adverse policy prescriptions on banks and when something goes wrong blame bank employees who implemented the policy.

Savers are openly talking about positive returns (net of inflation) for their bank deposits and safety of their hard earned savings in the context of rising NPAs in banks.

Those who borrow from banks have started analyzing cost-benefit aspects as they feel, the enforcement of credit discipline up to recovery could be more efficient now.

Expression of Solidarity

I would like to view the Ordinance amending B R Act as an expression of solidarity by Government of India for the initiatives taken by the Reserve Bank of India to restore the health of the Indian Financial System during the recent years. Vested interests have been relentlessly continuing their efforts to weaken the regulatory and supervisory apparatus in the financial sector. Fortunately, GOI has, of late, started showing signs of having understood the role of an efficient, strong and professional central bank in maintaining financial stability for economic growth.

*****

Banking on Bankruptcy Law

Credit is just one component of the resources deployed in industry/business and the prospects of the activity generating adequate surpluses to recoup the resources for growth and recycling depend on several factors, beyond the scope of credit monitoring. Indian financial sector is going through a transition and as the responsibility of other sectors for the chaotic situation gets identified and fixed, the health of Indian Economy will be restored and economic growth will not remain just a jugglery of numbers. If banking system has 'stressed assets,' of a level higher than the tolerance limits, there are individuals and corporates who have gained in the bargain, who are making a last effort to get away by maligning the regulator and supervisor of banks. This time around, 'WE THE PEOPLE' are more vigilant and are watching the game closely.

The Insolvency and Bankruptcy Code (IBC) passed by the Parliament in 2016 is yet another welcome move in the direction of strengthening the existing legal framework to deal with insolvency of corporates, individuals, partnerships and other entities. Currently, Government of India (GOI) is supporting Reserve bank of India (RBI) in guiding the banking system in using the piece of legislation (IBC) to handle the NPA Monster which has been growing in size and age taking advantage of a slow judicial system with several hierarchies and bureaucratic hurdles. For the banking regulator and banks, the taming of this monster has become a 'now or never' challenge.

Closely following the passage of IBC by Parliament, the Global Credit Rating Agency Moody's Investor Services had observed that "India's bankruptcy code boosts creditors bargaining power against big borrowers."

Moody's also referred to significant infrastructure constraints to be crossed for the framework to be fully operational.

"The current weak legal framework for asset resolution has been a key structural credit weakness for Indian banks," Srikanth Vadlamani, vice president and senior credit officer at Moody's had observed, adding that "the proposed new rules address several key inefficiencies in the current resolution regime."

The background for a fresh legislation culminating with the passage of IBC was the ineffectiveness of the multiple overlapping laws and adjudicating forums dealing with financial failure and insolvency of companies in India. One of the fundamental features of the Code is that it allows creditors to assess the viability of a debtor as a business decision, and agree upon a plan for its revival or a speedy liquidation. The Code creates a new institutional framework, consisting of a regulator, insolvency professionals, information utilities and adjudicatory mechanisms, that will facilitate a formal and time bound insolvency resolution process and liquidation.

Equipped with IBC, Central Government constituted National Company Law Tribunal (NCLT) under the Companies Act which became functional from June 1, 2016. NCLT has one Principal Bench at New Delhi and Regional Branches at other ten major cities.

In mid-June, 2017, Reserve Bank of India identified 12 cases of high value bad loans for being fast-tracked at NCLT. During July 2017, Essar Steel, one of the 12 industrial groups affected by this RBI guidance approached Gujarat High Court, arguing that the RBI decision was selective, arbitrary and discriminatory and obtained a stay order.

Hasty Criticism

As is the practice, media and analysts developed stories quoting certain observations of the Gujarat High Court out of context and questioned the wisdom of RBI. Columnist Debashis Basu writing in Business Standard, referring to the context of the stay order, made the following observations:

- The supposedly bold action of the finance ministry and the RBI of going after the dirty dozen has turned out to be hasty, ill-considered, clumsy and legally questionable.
- Every High Court continues to have an open door to defaulters; the much-vaunted insolvency framework crafted by a bunch of legal luminaries and academics seems deeply flawed.
- It is only the first sign of how the new bad-loan resolution system will quickly sucked into a legal quicksand. There will be pile-up of cases and resolution will grind down to a snail's pace,

at least in case of larger accounts where speed is of essence.

Not clear whether the voice is of 'hope' or desperation or just a 'curse!'

A Different Perception

I believe, this season, Centre and RBI are interested in moving forward in the direction of clearing the stressed assets mess in the banking sector by doing whatever is needed to overcome the initial hurdles they are facing. Action by regulators and governments will continue to be subject to judicial scrutiny and where there is a will, always there will be a way. One need not get disheartened by the view taken by Gujarat High Court over the RBI's selection of top defaulters. Earlier also, GOI and statutory bodies in India have got over such issues by 'following legally valid procedures.'

Just as opening several thousands of schools has not helped India become 100 per cent literate, the measures taken in 2014 onwards will not extinguish bad assets of the banking system that fast. Showering abuses at RBI or discrediting every initiative by GOI and regulators to put in place mechanisms to resolve a long pending problem will improve the readership of a column or a newspaper. But when a government and the central bank are jointly making some earnest efforts to meet the challenges which have arisen from decades of pampering of the rich and the powerful by a political system, efforts to divert attention from the main menu could easily get exposed.

It would be telling the obvious, if one observes that more bad loans are on the books of public sector banks. But business share of public sector banks also continues to be over 70 per cent. Has anybody bothered to know why private sector banks did not try to penetrate into more geographical space and aggressively improve their market share in banking business, post-nationalization of banks in India? Answer lies partly in the concluding observation recorded by Debashis Basu in the above piece: "Deep vested interests of academics, lawyers, bankers and accountants, who would like to feed off a clogged system as long as possible." May be some from these categories have become rich and powerful and are part of the 'establishment' today!

The stage for the present GOI-RBI initiative to go deeper into the problems arising from accumulation of unacceptably high levels of stressed bank assets and their concentration in large industrial groups was set with the assertion made by Dr. Raghuram Rajan immediately after taking over as RBI governor in September 2013. He had observed then that 'promoters do not have a divine right to stay in charge regardless of how badly they mismanage their companies.' Rajan was making the point that loan defaulters need to pay a price. Till then, the problem of NPAs was seen as an issue arising from inadequacies in credit decisions by banks or laxity in regulatory oversight.

Magnitude of the Problem on Hand

The 12 companies chosen by RBI for fast-tracking bankruptcy proceedings, roughly account for a quarter of the banking system's non-performing assets, and naturally, are entities with large operations. Some banks/consortiums of lenders have acted on RBI's guidance and action is in progress at NCLT. As mentioned earlier the way forward may not be without obstructions or protests as the Indian Legal System has several hierarchies and despite all honest intentions, the recalcitrant willful defaulters will not come around without trying all options available to frustrate banks' efforts to recover dues from them.

Whatever be the final benefits to the economy, the follow up of action in respect of the 12 high value accounts will bring to public domain more details about the 'give and take' between corporates in the private sector and the banking system with tacit approval of the government and the establishment managed by political leadership. Many forget that in the entire economy, the only sector which is regulated and supervised on an ongoing basis is the financial sector, thanks to the existence of RBI with an institutional mind.

Essar Steel Case

Out of the 12 high value NPA accounts being fast-tracked for bankruptcy proceedings by NCLT, let us take just one relating to Essar Steel. When the case first opened and Essar Steel got a stay from Gujarat High Court, media and analysts did not hide their sarcasm about the inefficiency of GOI and RBI. As the proceedings progress, it becomes clear that the rich and the powerful are never shy about hiding facts and using legal loopholes to delay the day of judgment. The claim made in the Gujarat High Court on July 13, 2017 by RBI jointly with SBI and Standard & Chartered Bank that Essar Steel was not revealing the correct picture of its journey to the bankruptcy proceedings and (Essar Steel) was presenting the facts selectively need to be seen in this context.

Essar Steel which has reportedly defaulted on more than Rs. 40,000 crore of loans was also talking about an 'offer' it made in January 2017 to pay the loan amount 'at the end of 25 years at 1% rate of interest. About this offer bankers pleaded ignorance!

The Gujarat High Court, on July 17, 2017 dismissed Essar's plea against NCLT proceedings.

When the Ahmedabad Bench of NCLT resumed hearing of the insolvency petitions filed by SBI and Standard & Chartered Bank on July 18, Essar Steel sought more time to file its objections. Partly conceding the petitioners' argument that the 'defaulter company' had had enough time for preparing objections over the previous fortnight when the issue was before the Gujarat High Court, the NCLT allowed the company time for filing objections only till July 22 and placed the next hearing for July 24, 2017.

RBI Explains

In an interview given to Business Standard RBI deputy governor S S Mundra was asked about certain observations by Gujarat High Court like, "RBI is under the impression that now when jurisdiction of matters pertaining to company law has been transferred to NCLT by enacting IBC, the NCLT has to follow their advice and directions. This is a serious issue..." One feels that the institutional mind of India's central bank is more graceful and mature when media, judiciary and a host of 'victims' affected by the performance of mandated role by RBI comes out in public, with what can be perceived as genuine criticism to scathing attack. S S Mundra's response, 'the wording was an 'innocent oversight' should satisfy those who are still up in arms against RBI.'

It's Natural

Long monotonous arguments in the court rooms and a compulsion to write long judgments makes the bench occasionally stray away to make comments in 'jest' during hearings or include loosely hanging observations in decrees which are later quoted out of context by a sensation-hungry media or writers who want to make their columns interesting or spicy. Another such misquoted observation by the court was directed against the mechanism put in place by NCLT, which read 'those with professional degrees may not necessarily be competent to run companies.' That again should be skipped as another 'innocent oversight' in expressing their Lordship's views, as, when you point an accusing finger to an unidentifiable target, all other fingers go in the opposite direction!

Commonsense is Law

It is reported that on July 23, 2017, Supreme Court, exercising special powers, allowed Nisus Financial and Investment Manager LLP (Creditor) and Lokhandwala Kataria Costructions (Borrower) to withdraw from the proceedings before NCLT when both jointly approached after arriving at a settlement where the borrower had made a part-payment. The amount involved was over Rs. 40 crore. Apex court intervention became necessary as either party cannot withdraw once the insolvency proceedings get started under IBC. Though this may be a special case, one gets the comfort that, even today, commonsense is law and once convinced, courts won't hesitate to come to the rescue.

Banking System: Built-In Safeguards

Writing in The Moneylife (7–20, July 2017), R Balakrishnan made the following observations:

"One great thing the Reserve bank of India (RBI) has done somewhere in the past is to have a solidly high level of SLR/CRR (statutory liquidity ratio and cash reserve ratio). This gives a great cushion to the depositor. If the SLR/CRR were lower (currently the combined CRR/SLR is around 25%), the magnitude of lending would have been higher, and perhaps, NPAs would also have been higher. SLR are amounts measured as a percentage of deposit liabilities of a bank and are invested in government securities; CRR are a smaller percentage of these liabilities that is kept as a cash balance with RBI."

This also explains the survival secrets of the Indian Banking System. When a bank is not able to maintain SLR/CRR at stipulated levels, the regulator gets the first signals of deteriorating health of that bank. If a bank has lent Rs. 75 (Net of CRR/SLR) out of Rs.100 mobilized as deposits and 20 percent of the loans become NPAs, still 85 percent of its assets will be safe. The capital adequacy requirement is another cushion.

Role of Bank Credit

Credit is just one component of the resources deployed in industry/business and the prospects of the activity generating adequate surpluses to recoup the resources for growth and recycling depend on several factors, beyond the scope of credit monitoring.

Have a look at the regulatory and supervisory system that oversees the corporate sector. Just try to answer these simple questions:

- Do we have a costs, prices and income policy for major industrial sectors?
- Do we have a regulator or supervisor who tells us when funds borrowed/mobilized from public are diverted by a corporate entity for purposes different from those for which they were originally borrowed/mobilized?
- What is the level of involvement of owners in running the companies?
- To what extent corporates and political leadership are mutually dependent for survival? Does such interdependence affect the policy formulation at government level and pricing and marketing at corporate level?

The purpose is not to embarrass by questions. The idea is to draw attention to the need to discipline private sector, by forcing them to accept the need for self-regulation, as the taxpayer and managers of public funds (GOI and RBI) have woken up and the blame game which held public sector banks responsible for all the ills in the economy is getting exposed.

Public Sector Banks were just conduits the establishment used to plough taxpayers' savings into private sector which the rich and the powerful businessmen misappropriated using private companies as instruments. It is now for the authorities to track the flow of those funds and bring back whatever is retrievable. The Insolvency and Bankruptcy Code and the arrangements put in place under the legislation are steps in the right direction to achieve such objectives.

Transitional Phase

Indian financial sector is going through a transition and as the responsibility of other sectors for the chaotic situation gets identified and fixed, the health of Indian Economy will be restored and economic growth will not remain just a jugglery of numbers.

If banking system has 'stressed assets' of a level higher than the tolerance limits, there are individuals and corporates who have gained in the bargain, who are making a last effort to get away by maligning the regulator and supervisor of banks. This time around, 'WE THE PEOPLE' are more vigilant and are watching the game closely.

*****

Section V

Development Issues: Works in Progress

Gold Management in India

Gold is back in the news, this time, for a change, for all good reasons. Yes, I have the initiatives being taken by Reserve bank of India to restore the glamour of the yellow metal by making gold participate in the India Growth story in a proactive way, in mind while making this positive statement. The measures taken by government so far to reduce demand for gold in India have not been successful, partly because some of them like raising import duty were in the nature of fire-fighting or first-aid kind of half-hearted attempts.

The reported proposal of Reserve Bank of India to swap old gold in Nagpur vault with purer variety, if it takes off, will open a new chapter in the country's gold management. It is distressing to remember the 1991 'gold pledge' episode to save the country from a payment default when the forex reserves of the country had touched its nadir. Think of the agony of a central bank Governor being forced to 'ship' a small portion of gold in the central bank vault for pledging to draw a small amount of dollars. Even though the gold lying with Bank of England has long been freed of pledge, it was not considered necessary to physically ship the bullion back to India.

It should have been for valid reasons that opions like selling a portion of gold stock or borrowing dollars against 'stock' of gold would have been dropped. Let us forget all that. But, let us remember, if the stock of gold was of internationally acceptable standard, things would have been different.

Viewed in this context the proposal to swap some of the old gold lying in RBI's Nagpur vault since pre-Independence times, with purer gold, though coming late, deserves praise.

According to reports, while the primary aim is to improve the quality of India's foreign exchange reserves, the move would ease the supply of gold, even if temporarily, in the local market where duty barriers have given rise to smuggling. RBI is likely to follow a mechanism known as loco swaps in the global bullion market, whereby gold in one location is 'swapped,' or exchanged, for gold in another location without physically shipping the yellow metal.

The gold that RBI would give to banks in India could be of a slightly inferior quality compared with the 'London deliverable' purer gold that it would receive from banks in London. The banks will deposit the gold in London in RBI's account with Bank of England.

Eighteen years after it had pledged gold, in 2009, when Dr. Subbarao was RBI Governor, India bought 200 tons of gold from the IMF – a development that took many by surprise. Considering the smaller share of gold in the country's forex reserves – Gold roughly accounts for $20 billion of India's $315 billion forex reserves – it is necessary for Reserve Bank of India to augment the share of gold in the forex reserves. The present initiative, if it takes off, could go down as an innovative plan on forex reserve management and will make it easier for RBI to buy and sell gold in the international market.

Banks and Gold Deposits

Two major public sector banks, namely The State Bank of India (SBI) and Bank of Baroda have raised the issue of treating a portion of the gold deposits held by banks, as part of the mandatory cash reserve ratio (CRR) or statutory liquidity ratio (SLR). As these are loud thinking it is premature to comment on such observations. One view is, the question of reckoning gold for CRR may not arise and technically and legally, gold can form part of the assets required to be maintained under Section 24 of Banking Regulation Act, 1949, in view of the following position:

CRR is part of the deposits that banks are required to park with the Reserve Bank of India under provisions of the RBI Act, 1934. It earns no interest, and is currently at 4% of the time and demand liabilities of the concerned bank, while the SLR, at 22.5%(or at levels prescribed from time to time), is the part of deposits that must be invested in in cash, gold or unencumbered approved securities, valued at a price not exceeding the current market price, an amount which shall not at the close of business on any day be less than 20 per cent of the total of its [demand and time liabilities] [in India] under the provisions of Section 24(Maintenance of a percentage of assets) of the Banking Regulations Act, 1949.

Domestic Gold Stock

According to one estimate, of the world's exploited stock of 140,000 tonnes of gold, WGC has estimated holdings of gold by Indian households at more than

18,000 tonnes. Of this, around 600 tonnes form part of forex reserves held with Reserve bank of India.

According to guestimates, India's surface gold stock may exceed the value of total deposits of the banking system in India. Going by the reports about gold and jewellery worth lakhs of crores of rupees with temples and religious bodies, this may not be an exaggeration.

While overall stock position and central bank's holding of gold are not that impressive, our country imports around 800 tons of gold annually which is not a small quantity by any standard. When it comes to deployment of this precious metal to the advantage of the nation, the story is really pathetic.

Gold should be restored its status as store of value by making it tradable, secure and available in 'paper' form against actual stocks of pure and standard gold. Move towards this objective is necessary from the forex angle and from the common man's perception of the metal as a liquid asset and pride possession.

At the national level, it is high time, gold is accorded the position it deserves in the forex reserves management. Centre could also consider an arrangement, through RBI or any other duly constituted authority, to trade in 'paper gold' against genuine tradeable gold stocks. The proposed Gold Bank-discussed later here – may be able to provide necessary linkages and guidance for the purpose.

In India gold is popular for all wrong reasons. The fascination this yellow metal attracts in its ornament and dowry forms has brought about an aversion among the people in the country even to talk about gold in public.

From the retail investors' point of view, unfortunately, Gold Exchange Traded Funds (ETFs) of Mutual Funds are yet to become popular and really tradable and therefore common man is tempted to invest in ornament gold which has several negatives such as difficulty in ensuring purity, making charges and other invisible costs, security related issues and inadequate liquidity.

The legendary money-lender who is very much present today in a variety of attires take advantage of the helplessness of the common man by luring him with loans against jewellery at high rates of interest and till recently offered unimaginably high amount of loan against each 10gram of gold with the ultimate motive of robbing the owner (the pledged gold is sold or forfeited by the money-lender as the loan plus interest grows much beyond the real value of gold pledged in less than a year). This trend, hopefully, has been reversed with the recent RBI directive to follow prudential norms in regard to Loan to Value ratio.

Institutional Support: Gold Bank

The proposal to set up a Gold Bank in India to manage inflow and outflow of gold and gold-related transactions within the country has been mooted first seriously considered inside Reserve Bank of India during early 1990's and has been coming up in different forms and in different contexts since then. As there are strong lobbies in support of interested groups whose 'business' will get affected if transparency and regulatory overview become a reality in gold management and therefore are opposing the proposal, the Gold Bank did not reach the drawing board so far.

The present environment seems to be more congenial for reviving the initiative.

The Assocham has made a formal demand to the government to set up a Gold Bank and introduce 'gold deposit accounts' operated through scheduled commercial banks. The proposal goes well with the Reserve Bank's proposal to release part of central bank's domestic gold holdings with simultaneous procurement of gold elsewhere.

Considering the federal set up of governance and the role of state governments in enforcement of various legislations having a bearing on gold management, it is important to take state governments into confidence in the management of gold. Thus, the time is ripe for authorities to think in terms of dedicated professional institutions at the regional/state level, which will handle gold from a banking angle. The Gold Bank can act as the apex body which should be equipped with linkages for import and export of gold and gold products with borrowing and lending capabilities.

States like Kerala have successfully intervened in other similar sectors like chits/*kuris* and lotteries, which were also areas of exploitation by vested interests. Private players had to fall in line and function with discipline and self-regulation.

Future Course

Reserve Bank of India should persuade the new government at the centre to understand the significance of the treasure in the form of gold stock with institutions and individuals lying idle in the country and put pressure on the powers that be to plan for putting at least some 10 per cent of the domestic gold to productive use in the next 5 years. This will reduce the country's gold import bill by 50 per cent. This can be achieved by:

- Making a realistic assessment of gold stock remaining idle in the country.
- Providing incentives to holders of gold stock to properly account the stock with them.
- Making gold deposits with banks remunerative.
  » Introducing gold-backed financial instruments which are not dependent on imported gold (The tiny instruments now available in the form of Gold ETFs and gold coins are indirectly dependent on import and have not attracted significant investor-interest)
  » Bringing a portion of household gold stock by offering some instrument like 'Gold Bond' backed by government guarantee to return solid standard gold at the time of redemption which could be, say, after 10 years and a small return on the investment in the interregnum
  » Quickly arrange for infrastructure, technology support and linkages for gold refining and certification facilities of international standard
  » RBI and GOI could consider even deficit financing for procurement of domestic gold as this could be the beginning of partial 'Gold Standard'

*****

Universal Basic Minimum Income

Article 39 of the Indian Constitution mentions certain principles of policy to be followed by the State, including providing an adequate means of livelihood for all citizens, equal pay for equal work for men and women, proper working conditions, reduction of concentration of wealth and means of production from the hands of a few, and distribution of community resources to 'subserve the common good,' Constitutional objectives of building an egalitarian social order and establishing a Welfare State by bringing about a social revolution assisted by the State and have been used to support the nationalization of mineral resources as well as public utilities. Further, several legislations pertaining to agrarian reforms and land tenure have been enacted by central and state governments, in order to ensure equitable distribution of land resources.

Universal Basic Minimum Income

The proposal to accept Universal Basic Income (UBI) as one of the themes for the forthcoming Economic Survey should be seen as an effort to pursue further the spirit of the directive principles of state policy referred to above and re-dedicate budget exercise as a tool for ensuring distributive justice, which is a responsibility emanating from the constitutional provisions. Once the debate on UBI picks up, the various components of such a concept, adequacy of the present levels of minimum wage, the path towards 'living wage,' the relationship between wage and savings, savings and social security, wage and healthcare and education expenditure in low income groups and so on will surface.

So far, discussions on such issues were isolated or confined to academia or research efforts. For India, once the political leadership gets convinced about a realistic UBI, resources will not be a problem. One possibility is, some vested interests will hijack proposal of UBI to mix it with "unemployment dole," an unhealthy practice existing in developed countries. While this should be avoided, care should also be taken to ensure that where employment assurance schemes are implemented, the compensations should be realistic.

There are several pockets in India, including many in states like Kerala, local population has successfully eliminated poverty and come up with regard to crucial human development indicators. Attribute it to militant trade unionism or the color of the flags held by parties in power, the credit for this goes to the insistence by workers for a minimum basic wage.

Hopefully, the concept of Universal Basic Minimum Income, as the debate picks up, will result in healthy deliberations on the need for grassroots level improvements in income distribution to ensure sustainable economic growth. A pragmatic approach to sharing of wealth can reduce several security concerns world over and ensure better living conditions, not only for the deprived class, but for many from the rich and the powerful who feel insecure today.

Writing in The Hindu on September 1, 2016, G Sampath raised the question, "Do we need a minimum wage law?." He went on to explain the concepts of living wage, fair wage and minimum wage and debated the seriousness with which stakeholders are approaching these concepts. One has to concede that it is a farce to retain the concept of minimum wage which does not ensure an income for the worker (who works full-time) which helps him and his dependents survive with some savings left for the family's social security needs. The present levels of minimum wages ranging from Rs. 1,650 per month (Puduchery, agriculture) to Rs. 9,100 per month (The minimum wage of Rs. 350 per dium for unskilled non-agricultural worker announced by GOI in August 2016), do not reach anywhere near the cost of 5 components mandated by the 15th Indian Labour Conference (1957) which were:

i. The wage must support three consumption units (individuals)
ii. Food requirements of 2,700 calories per day
iii. Clothing requirements of 72 yards per year per worker's family
iv. Rent for housing area similar to that provided under the subsidised housing scheme and
v. Fuel, lighting and miscellaneous items of expenditure to constitute 20 per cent of the minimum wage.

It may be recalled that the Seventh Pay Commission had fixed minimum wage for central government employees at Rs. 18,000.

Viewed in the above context, GOI will have to concede at some stage the demand for some reasonable relativity for wages of the workers in the unorganised sector with the entitlements of workers in the organised sector having comparable responsibilities. Whenever specific issues relating to job security and compensation are raised by unions or external agencies in the context of human development indicators in India showing uncomfortably low levels in comparison with similarly placed developing countries, some sporadic initiatives are taken by Centre or state governments. One such initiative is the introduction of the concept of 'full-benefit fixed-term jobs' in the labour-intensive garment sector by Modi government recently (See box "Fixed term employment going to become reality" on page 64, Business Manager, September 2016). But, a comprehensive legislation covering all aspects of service in the unorganised sector is not yet thought of. To answer the brief question "Do we need a minimum wage law?," the answer is in the affirmative, as we need it to know the extent of aberrations and violations and for further refinements to think of a 'living wage' at the appropriate time. During 20th Century, we used Railway Time Tables to know the number of hours by which some trains were running late!

Time is opportune to revisit the prices, wages and income policy. If we do not do this, labour migration issues within the country and flight of skills and expertise from India may rise to unmanageable levels giving rise to several social problems. The revamp of prices, wages and income policy need to be done quickly and for making the processes transparent and findings and subsequent action plans acceptable for the stakeholders, there should be meaningful debates in legislatures and with users of services of workers.

Strikes like the one on September 2, 2016 should be seen as symptoms of growing labour unrest and should be an 'eye opener' for initiating corrective action. Protests like this should not be evaluated on the basis of success and failure or losses and gains. Simmering discontent in the workforce emanating from the feeling that there is exploitation by the users of services, taking advantage of the helplessness of the workers, affect productivity and can have long term negative impact on economic growth. Sooner the governments and corporates amend the present approach, the better for the country.

*****

Agricultural Income Tax

In a well researched article captioned "Think beyond loan waivers" published in The Hindu on July 20, 2017 Ramesh Chand and S K Srivastava discussed in some detail the politics and economics of loan waiver with focus on agricultural sector. Hopefully, the issues raised by them in the article will also get some audience at NITI Aayog to which both of them presently belong.

It is high time the 'religious taboo' in India on taxing agricultural income is removed and agriculture is brought into the mainstream as an activity on which majority of the people of India depend for their sustenance. Going by traditional definition, a **tax** is a mandatory charge or some other type of levy imposed upon a taxpayer by a state in order to fund various public expenditures.

Methods of taxation has undergone drastic changes from the second half of last century and concepts like tax-less society and interest-less banking are being experimented. Simultaneously, efforts are on to make projects and sectors financially self-supporting. For the limited purpose of considering whether in India, agriculture as a sector is, or can be made, self-financing, let us discuss the possibility of taxing affluent farmers to start with.

The need for farm loan waiver is a product of several factors which together make farming a loss-making proposition for owners of agricultural land with landholdings of few cents to thousands of acres of land. These obstructive factors include, from high cost of inputs to low farm gate prices, absence of irrigation facilities and inadequate availability of electricity and transport arrangements, reluctance to promote joint farming where landholdings are small, expectations generated by government and financial sector about availability of 'cheap' credit followed by 'waivers' and so on.

There were situations in states like Kerala when farm credit obtained on the basis of landholdings directly went to fixed deposit accounts of borrowers with another bank next door and the credit availed became eligible for interest subsidy for prompt repayment, without involving any farming activity!

There is one more school of thought which genuinely feels that loan waivers have been tools in the hands of ruling parties to strengthen their electoral bases. Arguing on these lines, responding to the Hindu article mentioned above, one S K Meena wrote:

"It is important to highlight the sociology of poverty to understand the motives of ruling parties in waiving loans of farmers. From a functionalist perspective, having a substantial portion of the masses trapped in poverty gives the political leaders a much needed agenda and it gives bureaucracy a way to make itself relevant by making and implementing various poverty alleviation schemes..."

Irrespective of the irrelevance of the line of argument in a democracy, the issues raised are thought-provoking. There are vested interests which want agriculture to remain a loss-making activity and agricultural workers or small farmers to remain poor. To break the impasse, government has to make efforts to source funds needed to be spent in agricultural sector, including for subsidies and waivers from within the same sector. Here, a practical option is to tax agricultural income above a pre-decided threshold level.

If still consensus on agricultural income tax is unthinkable, there should be some arrangement for pooling a portion of surpluses from farm sector during good times and using it in bad years as also a compulsory crop insurance scheme covering all major crops. Insurance is about cross-subsidization.

Of course, better agricultural practices supported by technology should go side by side with all these efforts.

*****

Politics and Economics of Farm Loan Waiver

Uttar Pradesh state government's announcement of farm loan waiver (2017) amounting to Rs. 36,359 crore last month has given another dimension to the already messy environment in which India's banking sector had landed in recent years due to rising stressed assets across sectors. The genuine fear of bankers is that the UP waiver will be followed with similar announcements by other states, vitiating the credit environment in rural India.

During the Reserve Bank of India's customary media interaction that followed the first Bi-monthly Monetary Policy Announcement during the Financial Year 2017–18 on Thursday, April 6, 2017, RBI Governor expressed displeasure over the current spate of farm loan waivers by state governments and said these adversely affect the culture of repayments as well as put a severe burden on the exchequer.

When asked, "What do you think are the implications of the farm loan waiver schemes and is it a cause of concern for the RBI?" Dr. Urjit R Patel responded thus: "There are several conceptual issues, if one were to put one's hat as an economist on. I think it undermines an honest credit culture, it impacts credit discipline, it blunts incentives for future borrowers to repay, in other words, waivers engender moral hazard. It also entails at the end of the day transfer from tax payers to borrowers. If on account of this, overall Government borrowing goes up, yields on Government bonds also are impacted. Thereafter it can also lead to the crowding out of private borrowers as higher government borrowing can lead to an increase in cost of borrowing for others. I think we need to create a consensus such that loan waiver promises are eschewed, otherwise sub-sovereign fiscal challenges in this context could eventually affect the national balance sheet."

Dr. Urjit Patel was in fact repeating the consistent stand of the institution he represents. Since the massive waiver of loans in agricultural and rural credit sectors under the central government sponsored Agricultural and Rural Debt Relief Scheme (ARDRS), 1990 under which the responsibility for repayment of overdue loans in rural areas was shared by central and state governments, RBI has been pointing out to the central and state governments the implications of such waivers on the credit discipline on which the business of banking is dependent for survival.

Concerns expressed by RBI Governor now, echoes the gist of RBI's consistent stand on loan waivers which was articulated on several occasions since 1990. Centre and state governments, on most of the occasions, went ahead with their political agenda of such waivers which are partly responsible for spread of the malignancy of financial indiscipline to other sectors.

This time around, RBI has given the message loud and clear and the reference to 'national balance-sheets' should wake up the authorities responsible for policy formulation and opinion makers to the reality of the situation. When taxpayers' money is diverted to purposes other than those for which taxes are collected and budgeted, governments will have to borrow to meet the extra burden which will create imbalances in fiscal management. Many popular schemes like 'freebies,' tax concessions to corporates, and refusal to bring certain sectors like agriculture within tax net are already making the budget exercises at Centre and states level slip out of the accepted contours of financial discipline.

While RBI advice to move towards a consensus to eschew politically motivated agricultural loan waivers is timely and welcome and needs to be taken seriously, simultaneous efforts are necessary to provide relief to genuine borrowers. Such supports would include providing crop insurance, ensuring all linkages for getting timely inputs at reasonable costs, irrigation facilities, cost-related farm gate price, storage and transport facilities for perishable farm products and so on at reasonable costs.

Long Term Implications

The measure (waiver) has significant long-term implications for the economy which include:

a) Creating a moral hazard among borrowers as it removes any incentive for repayment. An economy already burdened with the problem of bad loans can ill afford such a systemic undermining of its credit culture and will adversely affect RBI's monetary policy initiatives.

b) Political situation in India is such that, if one state government extends a benefit to a category of beneficiaries, irrespective of the need or affordability, other state governments are forced to either offer similar benefits or lose political ground.
c) Such measures adds to government debt that will compel them to borrow more. Rising government debt which will add to the inflationary pressure and can frustrate RBI's desperate initiatives to keep inflation within mandated levels.

Blame on RBI Misplaced

The media and analysts in the recent past had been gossiping that the new RBI Governor Urjit Patel toes GOI line and in the process RBI's image has suffered. Recent months saw even books being released explaining how the credibility of the central bank is getting affected over a period of time. Relationship issues between GOI and RBI are getting magnified in books like "Dialogues of the Deaf" (TCA Srinivasa Raghavan) published recently.

RBI has taken the criticism unleashed, especially in the context of alleged lapses in post-Demonetization currency management in its stride. The approach of RBI to issues and how the central bank is playing its assigned role are being brought out on an ongoing basis in documents published by RBI. The first Monetary Policy Statement for the year 2017–18 and the Team RBI's interaction with media following the release of the document give enough indication that RBI's

Think Tank (which now includes eminent members of Monetary Policy Committee) does its job with professionalism.

A Piece of History

As state governments which have announced 'waiver' are unlikely to retreat from their position, let us look back and think of how best to avoid past mistakes in implementation of such schemes.

On March 5, 2013, a story in a mainstream financial daily made the following observations about implementation of a farm loan waiver scheme (Rs. 52,000 crore) by the then United Progressive Alliance government in 2008–09 quoting a report of the Comptroller and Auditor General (CAG) tabled in Parliament during the first week of March 2013:

a) The scheme, meant to help indebted farmers in districts where suicides occur, was so haphazard and faulty in implementation that no records were maintained of farmers' applications accepted or rejected by lending institutions or how many farmers were given fresh loans as a result of debt waiver/relief.

b) Several ineligible farmers were favoured and a large number of deserving small and marginal farmers left out in the implementation of the scheme.

c) CAG report said that the monitoring of the scheme was 'deficient' and there was even prima facie evidence of tampering with, overwriting and alteration of records, besides several other irregularities in implementation of the scheme.

d) The report observed that in the absence of monitoring of the scheme, lending institutions did not issue debt waiver relief certificates to eligible beneficiaries. Such procedural lapses resulted in achieving the original purpose of implementing the scheme.

It may be recalled that the Agricultural Debt Relief Scheme (ADRS) launched in May 2008 targeted to support 3.69 crore small and marginal farmers and 60 lakh other farmers in Maharashtra, Andhra Pradesh and Kerala (states from which several farmers suicide cases were reported in that year) to become eligible for fresh loans.

A post mortem report coming after a lapse of 5 or more crop cycles after implementation of the scheme may not help the beneficiaries of ADRS, 2008. Still, remembering past experiences may help in avoiding same or similar lapses while implementing the present scheme.

We Have a Sound Institutional Structure

At the highest policy level, agricultural and rural credit structure is the most well-researched and supported institutional arrangement in India during the post-independence days, till the emergence of LPG (Liberalisation-Privatisation-Globalisation) regime in India, circa 1990. That period saw massive surveys and studies like All India Rural Credit Survey, All India Rural credit Review, Agricultural Credit Review Committee and CRAFFICARD to mention a few. There were historic changes in the institutional structure also, like establishment of State Bank of India, Agricltural Refinance Corporation, application of Banking Regulation Act to cooperative banks and setting up of NABARD and Regional Rural banks.

Moving Forward

From mid-1980's, the policy focus shifted from farming and rural sector which continue to be the foundation and backbone of Indian Economy to more lucrative commercial sectors. Time is running out for a reversal of this policy shift. Such a reversal of policy approach will have to factor in:

a) A comprehensive farming plan based on the consumption, industry and export needs of farm produce.
b) Linkages like electricity, water, storage and transportation facilities.
c) Ensuring a pricing and crop insurance scheme which take care of cost-effective farming and several risks associated with farming.
d) At bank level, an appraisal and monitoring system from disbursement to recovery. Perhaps, the three component formula of olden days (Cash, Kind and Consumption needs) and "project Approach" in lending to agriculture may have to be reintroduced with appropriate modifications with changing needs.
e) Last, but not the least, subsidy is not a bad word. Where necessary, funds should be generated from surpluses in farm income and used for providing need-based subsidy. The present practices of interest subsidy for prompt payment and 'free electricity,' 'free fertilizers' etc should be eschewed.

*****

National Pension System

The PFRDA Chairman in a an interview given to a mainstream newspaper in January 2015 made some observations about implementation of National Pension System. Unfortunately, there was no further media debate on the subject. Views with reference to some specific observations by the Chairman are followed by a review of the genesis and status of NPS.

PFRDA Chairman's Observations and Comments

Quote:

The passage of the Pension Fund Regulatory and Development Authority (PFRDA) Act, 2013, in September, 2013 and its subsequent notification in February, 2014 was a major milestone in the history of pension reforms in the country. Armed with statutory powers, PFRDA has the mandate to develop, promote and regulate the pension industry with its flagship programme, National Pension System (NPS), to serve the retirement needs of the people.

Comment:

PFRDA came into being long after NPS was introduced and at this point of time, the authority has no elbow-room to reverse history. NPS (introduced as New Pension Scheme through a notification ten years earlier) was brought into being, by a government which was evading reality and was shy of speaking out truth. There were 'external' pressures to fund the defined payment pension scheme, the liability under which was (and even now is) being met on a "Pay As You Go" basis. According to a conservative estimate in 2006, the unfunded liability under the scheme was Rs. 3.65 lakh crore (It is incidental that the unfunded liability of pension funds in US was around $4 trillion, about one-fourth of that country's debt!) GOI gave an impression that the old pension scheme has been replaced by NPS. As defence employees were not covered by NPS and the outgo under the old pension scheme would continue for the next 30 years, GOI was saved only because of the illiteracy of the opposition and helplessness of those affected as the NPS was prospective in effect.

Quote:

The Act has given us statutory powers. We are now in a position to implement different variants of NPS and enforce their implementation.

We are now finalising many regulations, which will give teeth to the Act. There are about 15 regulations currently under drafting.

Comment:

PFRDA has no choices to make. It has to regularise what has been done without much statutory or legal backing.

Quote:

Overall, we have opened about 80 lakh accounts with a corpus of Rs. 73,000 crore. There are four variants of NPS.

We have one scheme for central government employees (except armed forces), the first one to get launched. All Central government employees are members of NPS. We have now over 17 lakh Central government staff covered under the scheme.

Comment:

After 10 years, per account balance is less than one lakh rupees.

Quote:

The second one is for State government employees and we have about 23 lakh employees enrolled. We have been seeing very good growth in this category and they actually surpassed the number of Central government subscribers. And, 27 out of 29 States have joined NPS. Tripura and West Bengal are yet to join.

Comment:

Many states have not started implementing NPS. In some states employees have been denied the EPF membership and government has not started contributing to NPS.

Quote:

The third variant is Swavalamban introduced in 2010 for the unorganised sector. Under this category, we have over 35 lakh subscribers with a corpus of Rs. 1,500 crore.

Comment:

Here, the per account balance is about Rs. 4,200 after four years including the per account contribution of Rs. 1,000 per annum by government. Future of such a scheme need not be discussed.

Quote:

"But one thing that is preventing faster enrolment is the fact that we still do not enjoy the EEE status, which employee provident fund (EPF) and PPF schemes have. [EEE status (exempt-exempt-exempt in income tax jargon) refers that money deposited in EPF or PPF schemes is exempted from income tax under section 80C; any interest or returns earned during the accumulation phase is also exempted from income tax; During withdrawal (after maturity) the money one gets is also exempted from income tax].

We have taken this up very strongly with the government to permit EEE status for NPS as well. We are hopeful that the upcoming budget will talk about this subject."

Comment:

Till things are sorted out, why not encourage public to continue with PPF?

Quote:

"Presently, only about 12 per cent of the working population is covered by any form of pension scheme. But most of the people covered by pension schemes are in the organised sector, that is, people working in manufacturing firms, civil servants and defence sector. But, the unorganised sector is more or less totally uncovered except those who have come on board under Swavalamban, which has been launched to cater primarily to economically disadvantaged sections of the society.

The scope for growth in this category is enormous. Because, we have about 40 crore people in the unorganised sector and majority of them have no access to any formal system of old age pension security."

Comment:

If this is the position after 10 years of implementation of NPS, where is the guarantee that things will improve?

National Pension System, Genesis and Present Status

The New Pension Scheme (NPS) was born 'unpopular' in December 2003(implemented effective January 1, 2004 through an executive order) and if the scheme in its new form (National Pension System) remains unpopular after Jupiter had another round-almost twelve years after introduction. It is time to have a review about the need to continue the scheme, as several mutual funds and Employees Provident Fund Organisation can together run schemes of the type under NPS professionally and much efficiently. Only, legal issues may have to be sorted out.

The captive clientele created by government by imposing the scheme on new entrants to government service and in government-controlled public sector is a frustrated lot. Both central and state governments are finding it difficult to meet the paltry 10 per cent employer's contribution. How much of the fund collected have reached fund managers and when is an issue to be probed into. The best option is to cover post-December 2003 entrants to service also under the pension scheme available for others including the entire defence staff.

For those outside regular employment and are interested in building a corpus for post-retirement life, organisations like Life Insurance Corporation of India, the Employees Provident Fund Organisation and private mutual funds should be asked to join hands and formulate appropriate user-friendly schemes. The one thousand rupees per member per annum being offered to new NPS members should be diverted to make such schemes viable and popular.

The Pension Funds Regulations and Development Authority (PFRDA) Bill, 2011 was passed by Rajya Sabha on September 6, 2013. The bill had been passed in the Lok Sabha on the previous day. Thus, it took about a decade for the scheme which was under implementation across the country and was being administered by the Pension Fund Regulatory and Development Authority which has been functioning under 'executive authority'(read 'without legislative mandate') to get a legitimacy of sorts. Beyond that, the legislation did not bring much solace either to the employees covered by the New Pension Scheme (rechristened as National Pension System – the abbreviation 'NPS' describes both) or the 90 per cent work force not earlier covered by any pension scheme for whose benefit NPS is being allegedly introduced and whose brief the media is holding.

The Main Features and Architecture of the National Pension System can be summarised as under:
- The National pension system would be based on defined contributions. It will use the existing network of bank branches and post offices etc. to collect contributions. There will be seamless transfer of accumulations in case

of change of employment and/or location. It will also offer a basket of investment choices and Fund managers. The National pension system will be voluntary.
- The system would, however, be mandatory for new recruits to the Central Government service (except the armed forces). The monthly contribution would be 10 percent of the salary and DA to be paid by the employee and matched by the Central Government. However, there will be no contribution from the Government in respect of individuals who are not Government employees. The contributions and returns thereon would be deposited in a non-withdrawable pension account. The existing provisions of defined benefit pension and GPF would not be available to the new recruits in the central Government service.

In addition to the above pension account, each individual can have a voluntary tier-II withdrawable account at his option. Government will make no contribution into this account. These assets would be managed in the same manner as the pension. The accumulations in this account can be withdrawn anytime without assigning any reason.

- Individuals can normally exit at or after age 60 years from the pension system. At exit, the individual would be required to invest at least 40 percent of pension wealth to purchase an annuity. In case of Government employees, the annuity should provide for pension for the lifetime of the employee and his dependent parents and his spouse at the time of retirement.

The individual would receive a lump-sum of the remaining pension wealth, which she would be free to utilize in any manner. Individuals would have the flexibility to leave the pension system prior to age 60. However, in this case, the mandatory annuitisation would be 80% of the pension wealth.

- There will be one or more central record keeping agency (CRA), several pension fund managers (PFMs) to choose from which will offer different categories of schemes.
- The participating entities (PFMs, CRA etc.) would give out easily understood information about past performance & regular NAVs, so that the individual would able to make informed choices about which scheme to choose.

The Defined Contribution-based New Pension Scheme (NPS) has replaced the Defined Benefit-based Pension Scheme and has been made compulsory for central government staff (excluding defence personnel, in the first stage) joining service from January 1, 2004. A slightly different version of NPS, somewhat similar to retirement benefit schemes offered by Mutual Funds has also been thrown open for subscription to the public. This article takes a view of NPS for central government employees and being gradually introduced by public sector organisations including banks.

Before the introduction of the New Pension Scheme through the budget announcement of 2003–2004, the major pension/retirement benefit schemes in operation, in addition to the Defined Benefit-based Pension Scheme which was available for government and public sector employees, were:

- Government Pension Scheme administered by central and state governments, financed through budgetary provisions.
- General Provident Fund out of employees' contributions. Open to government employees.
- Employees Provident Fund Scheme for employees in firms with 20 or more employees and Employees Pension Scheme, both envisaging contributions by employee and employer.
- Public Provident Fund maintained with State Bank of India, select Post Offices and other designated banks. Open to all individuals.
- Annuity schemes marketed by insurance companies including LIC.

The Central government employees who were in service as on December 31, 2003 have a Defined Benefit Pension Scheme. According to a 2006 estimate, the net present value of the pension liabilities of central government now being met on a *Pay As You Go* basis was Rs. 3,35,628 crore (6th Pay Commission Report, 2008). Considering this staggering liability which grows proportionately with rise in inflation rate and periodical revision in pay structure, Central Budget, 2003–04 contained a proposal to introduce the new restructured defined contribution pension system for new entrants to central government service. The New Pension Scheme (NPS) for new entrants to central government service from January 1, 2004, except to Armed Forces, in the first stage, replacing the existing system of defined benefit pension system was introduced through a notification dated December 22, 2003.

For those who get unduly perturbed by the pension liability of government, a word of solace comes from the following media report about Pension System in the United States:

"Using a more conservative method of accounting for financial gains in the marketplace, there is a $4.1 trillion gap between assets and liabilities — known as the "unfunded liability" — of all state-level pension systems in the United States, according to State Budget Solutions, a fiscally conservative think tank that deals with tax and spending issues at the state level."

The central government employees covered by the NPS are two-way losers. One, the huge costs savings for the government in pension pay out by the switch over to the defined contribution pension system from the defined benefit pension system is a direct charge on the overall remuneration package this category of employees are entitled to. Two, they do not have a window to air their grievances in this respect because the loss is not immediately felt and the full impact of the change will be felt only after 30 years or so when those who joined the service in January 2004 start retiring. It is also true that the anticipated savings in pension expenditure will also start accruing to government only by then.

A time tested social security arrangement available to a section of employees has thus disappeared without any alternative system in place. When one refers to social security arrangement, one has in mind all pensionary benefits including family pension. While in the private sector and profit making public sector undertakings employees have an opportunity to bargain and settle remuneration based on their skill and market realities, government employees and those employed in quasi-government and statutory bodies are a helpless lot whose bargaining power is stifled in the name of public interest. It is in this context that they deserve a special treatment at least in respect of social security arrangements like pensionary benefits.

The conscious exclusion of the category of employees covered by the NPS from the Sixth Pay Commission's purview while referring pensionary benefits for the Commission's review made it unnecessary for the Commission to even examine the impact of the change in the pension eligibility in the overall remuneration package of this category of employees. It is another matter that because the introduction of NPS was at a time the Indian Equities Market was performing fairly well, there was a general feeling that pension funds are going to bring attractive returns. The 8 per cent return given by government on pension funds so far, speaks volumes in this regard.

Till 2009, there was no thought in the minds of authorities about the arrangements for payment of compensation/Family Pension to the survivors of central government employees who joined service on or after January 1, 2004 and died in harness. When several such cases came up, as an afterthought, in 2009, Centre made some interim arrangements in this regard and decided to make provisional payment of Family Pension to such survivors under Rule 54 of the Central Civil Services (Pension) Rules, 1972. Such payments were subject to an undertaking to be furnished by the pensioner 'to refund or adjust the provisional payments......out of the final entitlements as sanctioned by the Government at a future date.' Such uncertainty and imposition of future liability is unheard of in the case of pension payment.

The stated objective of reducing the huge burden from Defined Benefit Pension Scheme by introduction of Defined Contribution Pension Scheme is not convincing as the financial burden is unlikely to come down in the near future.

It will be imperative for government to address issues like family pension, reasonable return on pension funds and review the adequacy of the present 10 per cent contribution from government and employees to ensure a post retirement lifestyle commensurate with that the employees are used to, during their active service. It does not require much calculation to observe that in the existing form, the NPS will land the employees covered under the scheme, by the time they retire, in a very disadvantageous position compared to their predecessors who enjoy Defined Benefit Pension Scheme, as Government's own estimates show a much larger outgo than the ten per cent contribution envisaged under NPS, for meeting the pensionary liabilities under the previous scheme.

From the employees' side, a conscious effort to understand the scenario and factor in these concerns in their savings habits and also in future bargains of salary structure will be necessary.

As things stand now and the way in which NPS is being marketed today, no one can find fault with the general feeling that let alone NPS being a shelter for the worker not covered by any formal retirement benefit schemes now, it is posing a threat to existing established retirement plans in the organised sector. NPS has already dismantled defined benefit pension scheme in the organised sector. Its next target is the Provident Fund and pension schemes now being administered fairly satisfactorily by the Employees Provident Fund Organisation, as already there are talks about NPS subsuming EPF schemes.

Though government and to some extent the media have been marketing NPS as a solution for social security problems of future 'senior citizens' of India, it is common knowledge that the scheme was introduced through back-door to get over the impossible task of starting to make provision for an estimated pension liability of nearly 4 lakh crore rupees when 6th Pay Commission was finalizing its report in 2006.

Other than the new central government employees who joined service from January 1, 2004 and others (state government and PSU employees) for whom NPS was made compulsory, effective various dates thereafter whose contribution adds up to about 85% of the fund corpus, the receipt from the 90 per cent workforce outside the organized sector so far is admittedly too low and nowhere near the aggregate assets under management of Retirement Benefit Plans with similar features (except employer's contribution) available with UTI and other mutual fund/s.

All these point to the need for an overhaul of NPS to make it a really useful instrument for retirement planning. Otherwise, next generation will brand it a parasite which killed existing social security systems in India.

Epilogue

Details of studies, if any, undertaken by Government of India before introduction of NPS in 2003 are not known. In 2006–07, ING Group and Indian Institute of Management, Bangalore undertook a joint research on pension systems in India at the instance of ING Global Retirement Services. The findings are available in the form of a 588 page book "Facing the Future: Indian Pension Systems"(By David J W Hatton, Naren N Joshi, Fang Li, R Vaidyanathan, S Jyothilakshmi, Shubhabrata Das and Sankarshan Basu. Publisher: Tata McGraw Hill Rs. 625). One wishes, Government of India and PFRDA revisits the analysis contained in this book which has gone into the evolution of new pension systems in several countries in the world and the relevance of those experiences in the Indian context.

Facing the Future claims to "analyse the results of extensive market surveys, draws from the experience of industry experts and studies the different pension systems around the world. The book encourages thinking on the pension issues which will lead to a viable solution to India's problems."

The book could be a good reference base for HR personnel handling matters relating to retirement benefits as also for those students, scholars and analysts who may be interested in understanding the evolution and growth of pension systems in India and abroad.

*****

Role of Auditors

When the history of the first leg of LPG (Liberalization-Privatization-Globalization) reforms in India covering the period 1990–2014 will be written, after a couple of decades, the role of institutions like the Supreme Court, Comptroller and Auditor General (CAG), Reserve bank of India and Election Commission will be critically analyzed. These institutions made up for the lapses of the legislators and the executive and made possible the emergence of India Growth Story. History will remember with gratitude names like Vinod Rai, Raghuram Rajan, Seshan, Sam Pitroda and Sreedharan who became legends in their own times for the contributions they made to the causes they took to heart. Here we look at the role of auditors in protecting the country's resources and ensuring prudence in exploitation and use of precious resources for economic development.

India is a country which has viewed audit with respect and has integrated the audit function in almost all financial transactions managed by institutions including banks, government and corporates. CAG functioning with head office in New Delhi and offices in all important state capitals, about 2 lakh chartered accountants and offices of the state registrars of cooperative societies cover the organizations in government, private and cooperative sectors.

In his April 2014 message in the Institute's in-house magazine, CA. K Raghu, President, Institute of Chartered Accountants of India (ICAI)said:

"Let's Gear up for Effective Bank Audit

As you are aware, a healthy banking industry is the backbone of sustainable socio-economic growth in our country. However, I am constrained to note that our banking system is under strain because of mounting Non Performing Assets (NPAs), which according to Assocham study, is expected to reach 1,50,000 crore mark by end of FY14.

As the keepers of financial discipline in the country, this situation should worry us all the more. Given our training, exposure and skills, we can play a crucial role in reversing rising trend of NPAs and vigilantly keeping our banking system healthy. By lending credibility to their financial statements, audits and auditors have an extremely important role to play in building a resilient banking industry. As such, the exercise of Bank Branch Audit assumes paramount importance for the banking industry, the banking regulator, our members, as well as the nation as a whole.

Let's conduct these audits in the most professional manner keeping a broader national vision in mind. You will be aware that to help you to carry out this nationally important assignment in most proficient and 'value add' manner, the Auditing and Assurance Standards Board has recently released its 2014 Guidance Note on Audit of Banks. This Guidance note contains comprehensive guidance on the various critical aspects that the members need to be wary of while conducting Bank Branch Audits. Let's also ensure compliance with relevant Standards on Auditing while carrying out Bank Audit engagement."

This signifies the importance given to bank audit by the Institute of Chartered Accountants.

The Comptroller and Auditor-General of India is appointed by the President of India under the provisions of Article 148 of the Constitution of India. The CAG derives his powers under articles 149 to 151 of the Constitution. The Comptroller and Auditor-General's (Duties, Powers and Conditions of Service) Act, 1971 has far-reaching provisions empowering CAG to audit the accounts of almost all entities having any 'give and take' with government. In some of the recent rulings the Apex Court has upheld the CAG's powers to audit the accounts of organisations in public and private sectors.

The commendable work being done by CAG now, is not the brain-wave of Vinod Rai or his predecessor who have sharpened the tools of audit to make them effective in the present context.

Performance audit is a concept introduced as part of commercial audit carried out by the then Indian Audit and Accounts Department in the late sixties. The purpose was to go beyond mere checking of accounts and ensuring that each item of expenditure was backed by a 'voucher' and find out whether the expenditure from public funds actually served the purpose envisaged when the outlay of expenditure was planned.

In the years that followed, the scope of audit has expanded along with the growth in public expenditure, multiplicity of sectors and ever-growing size of projects and extending geographies. As the funding comes ultimately from the taxpayer, the difference between public and private sectors is also getting narrowed down. Suffice to say, when CAG comments on nation's resources 'sold out' to private sector, traditional accountants get a doubt about his jurisdiction.

India's resources including financial resources deserve a more dignified treatment. If government or political leadership feel that CAG or for that matter any of the regulatory authorities should not comment on the performance part of policy decisions by ministries, it is time the country thought about having a separate authority to do the job. GOI should set up a 'Performance Audit Authority' which should have powers and competence to act as a watchdog to ensure that public expenditure is insulated from pilferages and leakages of the kind that are coming out every day. The present efforts of CAG, commendable though they are, do not result in online corrective measures which alone can minimize plundering of resources. Healthcare, not reasons for death through post-mortem, is the need of the hour for the Indian Economy as a whole.

Sometime back, the Supreme Court dismissed a Public Interest Litigation (PIL), which argued that the Comptroller and Auditor General's reports on Coalgate, airport privatisation and power sector went beyond CAG's constitutional mandate. While dismissing the PIL, the Apex court re-emphasized the statutory mandate of CAG and explaining the processes which the CAG reports go through, clarified that, if the CAG exceeded his brief, Parliament will surely correct him and tell him that the methodology adopted by him for the preparation of the report was not correct. This prima facie innocuous observation by the court would not have attracted the attention the ruling did, but for the celebration of the Apex Court ruling on the Presidential reference on allocation of natural resources. On the Presidential reference as it was duty-bound, gave the court's view upholding the supremacy of Parliament on policy issues and in fact did not give any adverse view against any statutory body including CAG. During almost the entire tenure of Vinod Rai as CAG, the institution of CAG was being harassed and criticized for performing normal duties expected of the organisation, by a government caged by the rich and the powerful. Performance Audit has been a tool used by CAG since 1960's. What Vinod Rai and his predecessor had done was just to sharpen the tool by infusing expertise into the audit team. By training and educating cadres down below and bringing professionalism in the performance of audit function, they improved the functional efficiency of the office. If similar initiatives had come from his counterparts heading several government departments and public sector or statutory organizations, the agony UPA II government suffered during its fag end would have been much less.

The Apex court minced no words in clarifying that CAG is not a mere account-keeper. The critiques who were of the view that accountant and auditor should bother only about the accuracy of figures were, for reasons best known to them, pleading ignorance of the changes that had happened in the law and practice of accounting and audit and the reforms in the CAG's office brought about by Vinod Roy and his predecessor, who understood the post-LPG scenario better.

The present political leadership is the 'who's who' of the rich and influential class which has its own constituency interests to protect. We are heavily dependent on government's other arms like CAG and judiciary to come to rescue when extraneous compulsions force government departments and public sector organizations to misappropriate or divert public funds to the advantage of their masters or greedy corporates and individuals. The differentiation between public funds and private resources is getting diluted, as either public resources are freely flowing to private sector or the exchequer is becoming responsible to make good the losses incurred by greedy individuals across sectors by mismanagement of businesses they own or operate. The initial response from government spokespersons to any revelations in reports of CAG is on dotted lines these days. First, CAG has exceeded his brief. Then, all his presumptions are not right. Third, even if some findings have some basis, losses are not as huge as are made out. Fourth, and that is the icing (as in Coalgate), in the given circumstances, there were not many options as several departments/ministries were slow in decision-taking. To the total discomfort of the government, this time around, even the mainstream media which usually shows some eagerness to protect governments from disgrace, refused to buy the government story without riders (Remember the zero-loss 2G Spectrum story of Kapil Sibal which was initially swallowed by a section of the media!).

Some analysts in the media who were not so much aware of the strength of the institution (CAG), even expressed the fear that the CAG-government face-off in the context of 2G controversy could see another oversight institution fall by the wayside. That was far-fetched cynicism. In fact, the debate on 2G auction and CAG Vinod Rai's observation on government's credibility as were healthy signs of India moving forward to a participative democratic system. Despite the massive efforts by UPA II to play down the significance of CAG's observations relating to the losses in the 2G scam, the audit report did play a proactive role in creating awareness about the corrupt practices in government, and across public and private sector organizations. Rai was successful in drawing attention to the erosion of people's faith in government. At this stage of development, prudence demands that the average Indian should be credited with the maturity to understand that the statement had implications beyond Rai's own personal defense in the 2G report controversy.

The shock to some in the context of report after report from CAG with more and more revelations about corrupt practices can be traced to the refusal of government and media in publicizing the evolution of the institution of CAG which has been silently molding itself in recent times to meet the challenges of changing times. Destiny had put Vinod Rai as CAG at a time when the country needed a person of his stature in that position. His having gone through the thick and thin of finance ministry and certain other tough assignments gave him the analytical mind and investigative skill needed to expose mega scams. The remarkable achievements of the CAG during his tenure are more attributable to the interest shown by an individual in protecting public funds. To ensure that the same thrust on 'conscience keeping' continues, the present approach of the CAG will have to be institutionalized by providing necessary legislative and administrative support. CAG's role in protecting the interest of the country in regard to public funds is similar to the role of the judiciary in protecting life and property. This points to the need to empower CAG to cause audit of any transaction involving national resources and more importantly, to equip CAG's office for the purpose.

A large number of the people's representatives in legislatures continuing to be those who are rich and powerful in their own way and capable of managing politics and vote banks and not necessarily interested in the sound management of nation's resources, we are dependent on government's other arms like CAG and judiciary to come to rescue when extraneous compulsions force public sector organizations to misappropriate or divert public funds.

As CAG's audit is mostly a post-event affair and judiciary will take a view only when issues reach them after due process, media has a major role to play. With the exception of some financial newspapers and a few national dailies, media generally show interest in the sensation value of issues and refuse to take on themselves the burden of working like a watchdog and educating their readers/viewers about how the drain on country's resources affect their pockets and living conditions.

The changes brought about in the vision and mission of the office of the Comptroller and Auditor General in recent years are worth accepting as a model for adapting with appropriate modifications by other arms of governance in Centre and states. These changes in the approach of CAG's audit are consistent with the vanishing line between public and private funds as both originate from the nation's 'sovereign' resources and the hard work of its people. We should sooner than later come out of the legacy of British rule inherited by us which has drawn a clear distinction between the assets owned by the rulers (read public funds in the present context) and wealth with the private sector or individuals, individual families or trusts/companies formed outside government ownership. This distinction is causing several unethical practices in our country.

Sometime back while talking to media, Vinod Rai has gone on record saying that he was open to guidance and expert advice from eminent statesmen.

Central and state governments should join hands with CAG's efforts to ensure that the country's assets irrespective of the nature of ownership are not plundered by unscrupulous elements. When CAG's reports bring out glaringly corrupt practices or make suggestions for incorporating better practices to avoid earlier mistakes, looking at them from mere legal or accounting angle or defending individuals and organizations instead of learning from past mistakes, correcting them before further proceeding are not in the best interests of the country.

Performance Audit

Performance audit involves assessing whether government policies, programs, and institutions are well managed and are being run economically, efficiently, and effectively. This is a task of potentially great significance – at a practical level for citizens, and at a more abstract level for the health and vitality of democratic governance.

For performance auditing to focus on citizen trust in government, government audit organizations should be equipped to design their audits to focus on equity as well as efficiency, and effectiveness. They need to provide work that allows citizens and elected officials to exercise accountability for the use of authority as well as the use of funds. When selecting and designing audits, audit organizations should consider at least the following types of equity: costs, services, access and coercion. It is a matter of comfort that in the Indian context, CAG has evolved a system of Performance Audit which can meet these challenges effectively. But neither the present audit arrangement nor the regulatory and supervisory framework go beyond 'compliance' issues. When lawyers take charge of governance, laws get manipulated to suit the convenience of the masters who put them in charge of governance. It is in this context the concept of 'service audit' or behavior audit' becomes relevant.

Long back, Kiran Bedi told an interviewer that everyday, before going to sleep, she used to 'audit' her own interactions and activities during the day and satisfy herself that she was on the right track. This, she said, helped her to make necessary and appropriate corrections, where necessary, quickly. The service audit discussed here is expected to help institutions and through them the society to make online corrections in policy formulation and implementation. Two recent incidents shocked those who took those in authority when they said 'let law take its course' seriously.

One, the reported revelation that there was an apparent conspiracy between the CBI prosecutor in the 2G scam investigation and one of the accused in the scam. Two, in Kerala, the Director General of prosecutions advised the state government against reinvestigation of a sex scandal, despite the Apex Court having recommitted the main case to High Court rejecting a state government appeal. In both the cases, the public feeling is that individuals who took quasi-judicial/judicial decisions or gave opinion were guided by the support the accused garnered from the powers that be.

The institution of service audit should be responsible
- To take cognizance of biased decisions by public servants including those in private sector who either handle public funds, like banks which accept public deposits or corporates which mobilize capital and funds from public.
- To provide broad guidelines for formulating appropriate norms for a 'code of conduct' for such public servants.
- To conduct selective audits and bring out reports for government to frame appropriate policy to ensure that service providers and public servants do not hijack the law of the land.

The above suggestions are illustrative and once accepted 'in principle' government may have to cause a comprehensive study before considering an appropriate legislative framework to support introduction of service audit.

*****

Tourism: Under-exploited Potential

India, with a richer set of natural attractions than those many other countries have been capitalising on, ought to plan its tourism strategy with care.

In the third week of November 2015, our daughter Reshmy and grandson Vihaan went on a short vacation to Hong Kong. My wife Sudha and I had not planned any outing during the Deepavali vacation.

I had not visited Lonavala, in Maharashtra, and my 'awareness' about that place was limited to just chikkis (for which the place is famous) and its waterfalls. Not being very comfortable with online booking practices, I went and booked a two-day stay at a hotel there, through the nearest travel agent in Bhandup, Mumbai. Also reserved two seats in a bus leaving Chembur at 9 a.m. on November 17.

We reached the hotel by 11.30 a.m. With just 50-odd double rooms, the hotel had a majestic, palace-like look. They served only Gujju/Rajastani/Chinese vegetarian food.

The package for two persons for two nights, included all meals, and for Rs. 10,500, at the present level of prices, it looked inexpensive.

Day one, in the afternoon we hired a car and went around. Covered almost the entire Lonavala and some parts of Khandala. Chikki shops were everywhere.

Waterfalls were conspicuous by their absence! They say you should visit during rains to enjoy the waterfalls. Did they mean rainfalls?

About tourist spots. We skipped the Karla Caves and Bhaja Caves, as the driver of the car we hired told us, "aap log senior citizens hai. Udhar chadhna mushkil hoga"(you people are elderly. Can't climb up the steps there). The MTDC Boating Club, another tourist spot, was closed. Skipped Wax Muzeum, as we had seen enough of celebrities in wax formations, some deformed due to heat, in other places.

We visited a couple of dams, a lake, a temple (Narayani Dham), a couple of 'view points,' Sunset Point and Reywood Park. A word about Reywood Park. Several trees, a children's park and a pathway in a vast area make it a nice spot where one would love to spend some evening time. But, it was shabbily maintained (I should say, there was no maintenance), waiting for someone to buy the area at a throwaway price and convert into a 'resort of sorts.'

That reminds me our Wayanad tour of 2013. That district had been converted into a nice 'tourist village' in Kerala, by developing half a dozen spots including Pookode Lake, Edakkal Caves and Kuruva Dweep with international-standard cleanliness and facilities. When we visited Singapore ten years earlier, I had wondered why India, which has several resource-rich geographical areas with tourist attractions much better compared to what Singapore packaged and served us, was not taking advantage of the rich tourism resources. What we saw in Wayanad convinced me that just one District Collector with government support can do wonders in the tourism sector.

In India, I have had a glance of most of the State capitals in southern, central and northern India. From the tourism angle, I have visited parts of Kerala, Tamil Nadu, Karnataka, Maharashtra, Gujarat and Rajasthan. Outside India we have visited Dubai, Thailand, Malaysia, Singapore and Hong Kong.

I believe India has not exploited even 10 per cent of its potential in the tourism industry. I am not against the private sector or public-private sector partnership in any area. But in the Indian context, the nation has to have a vision about the kind of infrastructure that it needs, priorities about geographical areas that could be made attractive tourism spots, and the extent of support the government can give through guidance and policy support. Conscious government involvement is necessary to protect the interests of the local population and the environment.

Unfortunately, like posh multi-specialty hospitals in India which care more for the comforts of patient-attendants, tourism is being marketed in India as posh stay arrangements and guided visits to certain spots developed with the inflow of tourists in mind, some 'heritage tourism,' and lately several good and bad practices in the name of 'health tourism.' There is no holistic approach.

Here also Kerala stands out as a model, that can be further improved. Though blessed with a long sea coast, several rivers and waterfalls, backwaters, pleasant weather round the year and a number of spots where tourists from outside the country and many from the other States of India would like to spend their days, the infrastructure available to provide stay and travel arrangements is not very impressive. Guidance from the government as to the standard facilities to be provided in different categories of stay arrangements is conspicuous by its absence at the ground level.

Experience Abroad

When we go as tourists to other countries, joining conducted tours or reaching there on our own and availing the help of guides, chances are that we will be going to places that have been developed to attract tourists and may not see the places which the host country is not proud of. In India we give the choice to tourists and many of them land in places that are not very attractive or are not maintained with visitors in view.

In countries such as Thailand, Malaysia, Singapore and Dubai, tourism is not about staying in big hotels or resorts and swimming or playing games. Though the countries offer good hotel facilities for stay, they ensure that visitors move out and enjoy whatever natural and 'created' tourist attractions they can provide. In some of these countries, dead butterflies to tamed elephants and dolphins, all sorts of birds and wild animals, and traditional dances of the respective geographies and large aquariums attract tourists much more than the large shopping malls and long beaches, which continue to be the main attraction in some other countries.

Countries that are dependent on or are aware of the revenue prospects of tourism, market the tourist spots by providing necessary travel linkages, stay arrangements and above all keeping them neat and tidy with all basic facilities around. They provide advance information to the tourists about the options they have to select the kind of places they may like to visit.

The Indian media are not very generous in telling you about the history and heritage of neighbouring nations. China is painted in red and described as a 'communist' country. But those who have visited China or at least Hong Kong and places in the vicinity of Hong Kong will tell you the respect the local people there have for churches, temples (many of them Buddhist) and heritage spots.

Kerala Model

I am an old-timer. Naveen Tandon, who did a project on 'Developing a branding approach to overcome the negative image perception of Chhattisgarh' last year, as part of his Post Graduate Programme at IIM Ahmedabad (2016 batch), is all praise for the Kerala Model of tourism development: "When it comes to branding for tourism in India, the runaway success is Kerala and we could learn a few things from the Kerala story to have an idea about how States have rebranded themselves to occupy enviable spots on the tourists' map. Kerala went from being a budget travel destination to being the biggest tourism brand in the country. Branding has played an important role in this transformation with the tagline 'Gods Own Country' and a strong campaign focussed on targeting the affluent. The building of the brand preceded the building of necessary infrastructure. The building of the brand created the necessary demand for good hotels and other facilities for the tourists and other players."

Within Kerala, there is a need to formally promote 'Festival Tourism.' The Onam celebrations at the district and State levels, the Thrissur Pooram, the Aattukaal Pongala, Sabarimala pilgrimage, Theyyams in the Malabar area and several other Hindu/Muslim/Christian festivals are examples. If transport and stay arrangements improve, tourists will make it a point to link festivals in their travel plan.

Kerala has some artificial water parks. But we do not have a theme park of international standards. A couple of parks/entertainment areas will be useful additions.

Aranmula has all the linkages and resources necessary to grow into a large modern 'Herbal Tourism Village.' The concept could include participation of major Ayurveda entities. There should be facilities for stay and treatment for different economic classes including the Indian middle class and 'rich' outsiders. Development of medicinal plantations in adjacent villages is a possibility. Aranmula has the additional advantage of having two international airports within a distance of 150 km.

Kerala could indeed go places — provided a carefully charted out plan is put into place.

*****

SECTION VI
Prologue as Epilogue

Eradicating Corruption: Power to The People

Unless the people do not come together to oppose corrupt practices across government, public and private sector organisations, the present situation will get perpetuated. This is not an ill that can be cured by another institution like Lokpal or by debates in parliament *"...will transform India's 1.2 billion people into 1.2 billion opportunities"*

– Sam Pitroda,
25th September, 2012.

The current decade is an opportunity for India to come to terms with her real problems and bring about a change in direction, not allowing back-seat driving by external influences, making a path motorable for coming generations and showing the world that the country's inherent strengths and vision are intact. To make this possible, the fourth pillar of democracy, the people, should play their role effectively. The greed of the rich and the powerful is preventing this from happening. The modus operandi and culprit is corruption. Let us find out whether this issue can be handled, if 'people' come together. When the India Against Corruption (IAC) movement was gaining popularity, Education World, the human development magazine (September 2012) observed:

"The most common refrain is that Team Anna is a single issue movement which lacks the capability to manage the complexities of Indian politics. Such advice is indicative of the extent to which the intelligentsia is cut off from the public, groaning under the heavy burden of institutionalized corruption. Since unchecked graft in government cuts across every sector and segment of Indian society, by definition it is a multi-sector issue. The rotting grain mountains of the Food Corporation of India are the fallout of widespread theft and defalcations within the organization, which has prevented construction of adequate storage facilities; the country's ubiquitous urban and rural slums are the outcome of pernicious corruption in the real estate sector; mass illiteracy and unemployability of millions of youth is the result of chronic corruption in education, and poor health and nutrition of the general populace is also the natural consequence of rampant corruption in the public healthcare system."

Quoted here to share my comfort that awareness about the cancerous grip of corruption on society is growing and if the message gets conveyed in an effective manner in the education world in India, still there is hope of salvaging what is left of India. Our country's faith in resurrection from difficult situations is well-founded in the following stanza from *Bhagavadgita*: *Yadaa-Yadaa Hi Dharmasya Glaanir Bhavati Bhaarata Abhyutthanam Adharmasya Tadaa'tmaanam Srijamy aham (Bhagavadgita, IV.7)* (Whenever there is a decline of righteousness and rise of unrighteousness, O Bharata (Arjuna), then I send forth (create incarnate) Myself.) We have seen tens of thousands of such incarnations at Jantar-Mantar around Anna Hazare during the IAC movement and seen and experienced the support of millions of others through the media during those days. By selective targeting, the rich and the powerful have delayed the fight against corruption which will erupt in one form or other and engulf the corrupt wherever they hide, sooner than later. Let us consider a shortcut to bring the corrupt from their hideouts. There could be other methods which may work faster and better. But to initiate the debate let me introduce the idea of a domestic 'Corruption Index.' The intellectual leadership of India should take up a project to assess the extent of corruption in India. This could be done by scientifically evolving appropriate methodologies for having a 'Corruption Index.' There have been efforts to measure corruption with reference to various practices in different nations and rank countries according to their status in comparison with others in the group. But, one, it is no use knowing our position with reference to others and two, as we observed, corruption has more dimensions than illegal practices or bribes. As our government encourages 'self-regulation' these days in different areas, why not attempt a regulatory mechanism outside the statute book for assessing and quantifying corruption? It is here the idea of a "Corruption Index" gets significance. Imagine, one "Corruption Indexing Organization" (CIO) gives you a rating of the person, department, organization (including a political party)/institution on a scale of, say, hundred, how deeply sunk they are in corruption, based on parameters explained to you? There can be several such CIOs specializing in different walks of life. Of course, the functioning will be fee-based and independent of government except for overall regulation, may be through a registration arrangement. Let us consider a couple of areas where this can be tried on a pilot basis.

- **Candidates contesting election**

Candidates themselves may furnish relevant information to the CIO and get their index commuted. The parameters could be, accumulation of wealth during the previous five years and source thereof, attendance in legislative houses where the candidate was a member during that period, participation in developmental efforts in the constituency and pending cases/charges of corruption if any (list is indicative). Once stabilized, index could be worked out annually. **Government departments** Initially, the exercise could be confined to departments vulnerable to corruption. E.g. Excise, Motor Vehicles (Registration, etc) The parameters could be, number of complaints during the previous five years, pending charge-sheets/cases involving staff members, punctuality in disposal of cases and assessment based on internal reporting (again, the list is indicative). Periodicity for revising index could be annual. It may also be necessary to develop skill through introducing corruption as a subject in Management Institutes and other professional schools so that CIOs are able to recruit experts for the purpose of functioning with professionalism. Two years back, a national newspaper had, side by side, printed views for and views against corruption. One view was that corruption is the oil that lubricates the wheels of progress. Many seem to agree with this view. Very recently, I read in a magazine an observation attributed to Kaushik Basu, which said: "The rationale for corruption is economic; the best way to handle it is to legalize it." Perhaps, this advice from the one-time economic advisor to the prime minister has been taken literally seriously by powers that be. Sometime back, the Supreme Court, while hearing a corruption-related case, though sarcastically, had suggested legalizing corruption and fixing specific amounts for every case. Perhaps, our private sector has implemented this suggestion long back. Service charges levied by the banks are one example that comes to mind. Now there are banks which charge separately for opening of accounts, issue of cheque books, certifying that an account holder is maintaining an account with the bank, for not maintaining minimum balances in deposit accounts and so on. The government is following suit and introducing levies/charges for every transaction in government offices. It was Zail Singh (when he was president) who said that if an individual's assets multiplies manifold in a short span of time, keep an eye to see how the growth happens. Obviously, he had corrupt means used by people to become rich and it was inconvenient for the rich and the powerful to take notice of the observation. If Zail Singh had been taken seriously, even the doubling of value of assets reported by Dr. Manmohan Singh this year would have attracted scrutiny. Last week, in one of my online comments, I had referred to the four pillars of democracy. A friend asked me whether I had the fourth estate (media) in mind, while including a fourth pillar in addition to legislature, executive and the judiciary. I answered that I had "WE THE PEOPLE" mentioned in the preamble of the constitution in mind when I commented (frankly, the idea of accepting 'twitter' as the fourth pillar of democracy was yet to get currency!). Let us go back to the preamble of the Constitution, which reads: "WE THE PEOPLE OF INDIA, having solemnly resolved to constitute India into a sovereign socialist secular democratic republic and to secure to all its citizens: JUSTICE, social, economic and political; LIBERTY of thought, expression, belief, faith and worship; EQUALITY of status and of opportunity; And to promote among them allFRATERNITY assuring the dignity of the individual and the unity and integrity of the nation; IN OUR CONSTITUENT ASSEMBLEY this twenty-sixth day of November, 1949, do HEREBY ADOPT, ENACT AND GIVE TO OURSELVES THIS CONSTITUTION." The Constitution is given to the people of India and it is the solemn responsibility of every Indian to protect it. Of course, the agent of the people carrying out this task is the government. This has been made abundantly clear in the Constitution through a bunch of directive principles of state policy forming part of the Constitution and explicitly stated to be not enforceable by any court, but with a clear direction to government to apply them in making laws. I am convinced that unless the people, who do not directly participate in the affairs of legislatures, executive and the judiciary, those in the media and those who are part of these three wings, but are silent spectators to the goings on, due to various compulsions, do not come together to oppose corrupt practices across government and public and private sector organisations, the present situation will get perpetuated. This is not an ill that can be cured by another institution like Lokpal or by debates in parliament.

*****

www.ingramcontent.com/pod-product-compliance
Lightning Source LLC
Chambersburg PA
CBHW020739180526
45163CB00001B/283